Future and Modernization
of Afghanistan

Future and Modernization of Afghanistan

Sultan Masoud Nawabi

Rev. date: 06/18/2013

To order additional copies of this book, contact:
Xlibris Corporation
1-888-795-4274
www.Xlibris.com
Orders@Xlibris.com
129670

DEDICATION

Dedicated to my parents, Mohammad Naim Nawabi, Station Manager
of Afghanistan Airport Arina Air and Akila Nawabi, a medical nurse

February 26, 2013

I remember tow massive mountains close to our house in Kabul with that four season that Kabul, had, I liked specially the winter time going up in the mountain with other children, skating coming down there where beautiful dogs around to play with, the same in spring thee where wild roses in all kinds of colors, and spring water to drink from and shiny color full stones.

I was always curious asked questions; I was taking my school at that age very seriously, I remember my dad, he liked his party's a simple men with a good heart, worked in Kabul airport, in airline called Arianna Afghanistan air; he was a station manager in Kabul airport, mom was a medical nurse in some hospital in Kabul, as the family moved to Tehran Iran, I continued my studies in Tehran, my dad worked in a Korean company as an English translator, and mom was a medical nurse, at one of the hospital in Tehran.

As the revelation started our family moved to West Germany, learning German was not easy for me at first I have continued my studies as much as I could.

I worked in a restaurant, and after in construction projects, because my older brother, and most of my parent's family was here in US therefore we moved to US, I worked to make a living, and at the same time continued my studies as much as I could.

Because of financial reasons, I was basically home schooled, in the mean while god gave me a son (Sebastian) from an American girl friend who I love more than life.

Life did have up and down, but still I am thankful, god is kind, for some reason when you are born somewhere in earth you never can get to choose where you should born, but that is your identity, and pride mine happen to be the most tragic country ever (Afghanistan) war is war, but when you see those children with their faces dead looks like as they are sleep in massive graves, it is not tolerable for anyone, even if your heart made of steel.

You going somewhere in private, and brain storm the situation, and you can't do anything about it, and you are ashamed of yourself, your body temperature drops you are cold and you said to yourself why are you standing, and watching it like a coward?

You think what can you do about it, there is . . . nothing you can do, and you sigh . . .

Sultan Masoud Nawabi.

Future and modernization of Afghanistan I am writing this book because something is nagging me in back of my head to do this. I don't know when you born some were you never forget it. I was not from some rich family, but still you have that kind of obligation towards your country somehow. It doesn't matters what continent you go to people ask you this you don't look like you are from here. Where you are from. And you must answer and the answer is I am from Afghanistan they know right away who where the war is.

They look at you down and they change the subject and it hits you and you ask why I am from there. And you visualize the situation of poor children with torn cloths and their mothers crying and complaining about the misery of their everyday life from the sounds of bullets and bombs from sky. They are standing for hours with smile on their face so they receive a bag of corn shamefully. They take it and they are still hopeful towards future. How can you avoid thinking about that if we say help did not go there after 911 so many countries helped Afghanistan. First of all financially, politically now more than 70 countries army is there from the best countries around world. All of these NATO Soldiers leave their families and loved ones behind go there to help in a very complicated war. For an impossible people I am from there. I know who they are and the only way to save Afghans you have to save them from them self's is to have a strong leadership. As we all know bringing unity and to make Afghans responsible for their own home this Country is not easy.

Afghans speaks in two different languages, Pashtu and Dari and the majority are Pashtuns that's where the problem or genets because near the border with Pakistan called Pashtonistan and Keota also Waziristan these areas are almost lawless regions. The Pakistani Government has no Control over them. These areas are poor and they are against every one. They have their own law and regulations. They respect each other it is not so easy to understand their social mechanisms. They make their own guns and weapons as well they do get along with each other well and they respect their elders. They kind of create their own laws and social style. There is beast in them more like lions or tigers are they don't want to be crossed or they will attack you even if you speak fluent Pashtu. Coming from some other place you will not understand them well enough. They have honor code for them self's in there tribe any women or chilled will be safe even if they don't know those personally. These tribes are extremely religious. Any fanatics can come from the Arab world there with Islamic radicalism and money can have followers obviously one of them is al-Qaida and Lashker taiba and so many more which I don't know. Their names it is rapidly growing stronger for what reason beats me to take revenge from whom exploding yourself in hospitals where the women and children there for treatment. What kind of statement is that if political we have to sit down with a psychiatrist from Pakistan and ask this question what is that mean I believe the holy book has been rewritten by some Arab radical scholar to make these young men to do such atrocities in such violent way to make a statement and keeps every one wondering and confused for some kind of evil purposes that never goes away.

I don't know why god gave me this heart that I never ever can keep hate in to me accept in some of books they say there is an evil in every human as well as goodness. Maybe that can play lots of role into destruction of the world today. Pakistan has nuclear weapon or they calls it nuke these days. How dangerous that can be I am sure everyone knows. In Pakistan, president or prime minster has no authority's the powerful that makes the decisions are army so called ISI. They are playing games with western countries especially with United States for their financial and political gains so they can reach their own evil purposes. They are busy doing that for the past thirty five years now they are expert with it in a way they want to scare the west using a poor country Afghanistan with the 75% Pashtuns. Changing the holy book (Koran) by their own scholars and keep preaching what is for their own benefit to me that is the biggest sin in Islam as far as I remember. In Koran there is sentence that says if you kill one human being that means you have murdered the all humanity. There is a verse in Holy (Koran) and I are sure of it so there is a problem like this. What we do about it I believe first of all we should have a serious talk with ISI of Pakistan and shake them up. You and your government lied so much that you don't know what to lie about any more with every one let's make some serious changes in your policy making. Change the way you all are thinking keep on protecting the radicals helping them financially giving them all kinds of we pens killing innocent people to the point that suicide bombers is all over the place as we handstand seventy suicide bombers a day are send by Pakistan authorities to Afghanistan to destroy that poor nation. Enough is enough we shall stop them once for all, and seriously start the reconstruction of the nation as we all know there is the money to do so and there are more country's keep on promising that they will help our nation who helps us they believe in us like Japan that we are also honest hard working people but unfortunately that is not the case as we afghan know some of the afghans who has money they buy property's in Dubai and invest their money. Afghans because they feel safe there Dubai as all world knows is a rich Small beautiful country. They don't need our investments there is should be a law invented in Afghanistan that are Afghan Citizens 'shall not be allowed to take their money out of Afghanistan and invested to another nation, at this historic time that Afghanistan needs each dime to be used in Afghanistan the money should circulate in our country like our blood in our body. I am not saying the money should be taking away from people they should use it inside by all kinds of investments they can do with its growth from businesses be able to buy privately malls.

Construction Company's all of big businesses agriculture big company's making goods private hospitals clinics and so on construction companies and so forth. Our biggest example is West Germany I am sure you have seen on television or papers in history books somewhere or somehow in world war two they have been bombed like no country has been bombed before in history. I have been living there in my teenage years for almost four years or more. Whatever I looked at I admired it from buildings to high ways automobiles convenient metros or trains so not everyone has to drive there bridges they used their under grounds it seems like is another city's is down there. Opera shows how their brain works we all should learn and follow they were humans too. They spelt their blood to make it again they said we are Germans we are not going to give up. They made it and made their dreams come true; none of them said who you are from colon I am from Frankfurt so I am better than you are. It is not such thing in the western world so if we don't know than we must follow why there is a school a child goes to first grade he or she is so proud that they will learn something they want follow their books why because they want to follow the writer of that book. They come home and learn more from parent's television and their friends so we adult Afghans at this twenty first century we are all visual and hear thinks we never bother to read.

When some of us graduate from university we think that is it for me my obligation to education is over we only talk about it; constantly ho I have been graduated from that University we only study to pass a test somehow somewhere and oath to the god I would not read a piece of paper or a book again as we all know today's technology constantly is changing for the better. And that is our job to keep up with new technology computers and machinery's read it understand it and practice it that's how is going to be until the day we retire.

Every generation is growing up to bring some positive changes for the next generation that's why I am writing this book so when I die first of all I want to die young I hate to get old drooling in nursing homes. A young student may be read this book and learn from it that's why I am going leave this book behind for example we claim that we have our five thousand years history for the past three decades. I understand that there was a war let's remember 1970 what have we Afghans had at that time and accomplished before that may be you all thinking of

Kabul was ok there were another 28 provinces people. I am sorry to disappoint you nothing in five thousand years we are talking long time most of Afghanistan including Kabul we were lucky to have plate of rice a day. I understand we are poor nation. We don't have oil and lots of natural reassures which we all know we do we have us valuable stones and massive amount of coal in these massive mountains. Something has to be in it we must invite archeologist from around world and see what they can do and what their advice will be for us. So it comes to land agriculture everyone knows that we can do magic's with our land in agriculture more to think about it what we need is machinery equipment for agriculture to bring about the goodness of our land.

Make a difference so no one can complain about shortage of food again once and for all. All this is a very important issue that it has to carefully planned and implement and detailed with our partners around the world. Hunger should be resolved when a person has nothing to eat can he or she cannot concentrate on their daily lives specially children who go to school in the morning. Without a breakfast they cannot learn any subject with empty stomach. We have to take care of the basic but very important issues. First of all we need to fix the primary problems than jump on to the next issues and take a look to our kettles how they have been treated their health so on for producing milk cheese and in general poultry for the people.

Now I want talk about the treatment of women in Afghanistan ho my god how these men call themselves Taliban could do it to these young women cut off the women nose and hears and shooting a women under that blue burka as they shoot her in the hit hundreds of people sitting around as she is sitting down in the head that blue burka becomes bloody and her brain is demolished as these men called Taliban laughing with some kind of pride. I remember that cowboy western movie Clint Eastwood staring there is a seen Clint Eastwood looks at them in a duel and says it is not nice you laughing with that deep voice of his he looks up and he draws his gun and five of them are dead in matter of seconds. I always visualize that great scene.

I titled this book the future and modernization of Afghanistan in Islam. There is a verse that Islam must adjust itself with time. There always in the holy book education is something that each Muslim should pursue and live your life with prosperity happiness whatever in Islam we understand. God wants us to live an healthy clean life's a clean society men and women environment with the respect to each other of course I am not a scholar from Egypt or Saudi Arabia, but this is my religion as well I do know something's about it.

Today Muslim countries like turkey Indonesia Arabs and money Muslim societies are living In modernized states and going towards prosperity and Taliban wanted to live like 14th century. They even couldn't manage to do that when they came to power why don't you say I am a barbarian and I am getting a great pleasure killing people. I like to see people hanged, beheaded, tortured until the day I die reminds me of Johnny Carson he would of have said you are some mean people aren't you already than . . .

We Afghans must be united alert and wise not to get in to their trap again from north to south, east to west of Afghanistan if we want to have our sons and daughters above all the dignity of our nation and its future as they say as united we stand and divided we fall. The border with Pakistan called Border of Duran must be monitored twenty four seven with the highest technology and highest paid Army in that region we need that that is the only way possibly we can protect our country. Anyone tries to pass Duran border must be shot dead as a terrorist or without asked any question whatsoever. And the individuals who are coming legally should be investigated.

Not long ago few American civilians was working in the ministry of interior these people crossed the border. Bought an army uniforms and shot the civilian Americans as they were busy helping in their desk to the back of their heads they are smart they know how to blind in and do there evil acts and they have money I know for a fact where the money is coming from it is coming from drugs that they are selling harvested in Afghanistan plants called popes and the usual suspect Mr. .ISI or the army in Pakistan.

Well let's talk about America for moment. America now is not only super power she is super-doper power in the world and it is getting stronger by the day people wondering what is causing all these atrocity's the answer to that is Julesy being defensive people here are going on diets to lose weight while in poor country's overseas losing a child because of starvation in most of country's overseas. American military are stationed showing that kind of power to any home land America will be despised so in my view America shall play a role that can be like a rich kind father not to police the world but with acts of kindness show the third world how to improve themselves and be a partner in the world and help to improve the third world economy today third world countries is getting over.

Populated by the day each women wants give birth to over five children I remember tony Blair former prime minister of United

Kingdom did talk about this issue with a reporter he was saying we must take this seriously. Even in the western countries if the parents or single parent cannot take care of the child the way a parent should do financially and emotionally to bring up that chilled happy and prospers so he or she can help.

They and the Next Generation they should put stop to that or we should have organizations to help that child who is unwanted and feels deeply sad parents has major role in child future during upbringing of that boy or that girl. As they say in our language Farsi a mother with one hand shakes the crib and in other hand the World.

Now I must continue about reformation of Afghanistan, and its stability first of all we must bring some changes to the basic culture of Afghanistan the culture is extremely weak the way they general population thinks and has conversation with each other carry them must change for the better.

The custom what we wear there is a turban and the outfit that looks like pajamas in modern world they called them pgs. When you wear that the very first minute you feel so comfortable that you want to go to bed or rest or sit-down have a cup of tea you get in to a comfort zone you don't want to do anything and you feel lazy in general.

When you don't shave your beard leave it that long touch is you're Billy button and don't brush your teeth and take a shower only twice a month you don't feel so good naturally which is not healthy. We must change that once for all.

Dear afghans, now is 2012, king amen aula khan has said that in early 19th century every one said he is an infidel let's get him out of here. He is getting us out of our comfort zone he went to exile and he died in Rome

Italy. Peace upon his soul. That was 90 years ago. Was a bit early when is the right Time than.

I have a vision for what to wear daily so made by clothing company's different modern styles for different seasons and shoes or boots that it is light and protective of our feet good styles I will have. The show cases in some pages so you will see it for your selves. You might say why are talking about so money basics I have to, this is where we are begging to future and civilization of our country.

My idea for minister of education from first grade through college and universities and so on first of all I like to change the name of ministry of education from (mharef) comes from word mharefat. A child of fifth gather what would he or she knows about mharefat, to ministry of amoohzesh and Perveresh or simply call it ministry of education.

Because amoohzesh means learning, but perverse means to bring up the students with kindness to take care of their emotions, and every day challenges and helping their confidence for the future of the country as well as education. We must call on India to help us from the very first grade to junior High also high school and finally Colleges and universities with all of the text books and style of education. If we love their music and entertainment we must pay attention more and follow their education religiously and have extreme respect for it.

There is a book called the world is flat you must read the book has been rattan by an American author Mr. (Thomas freedman). India has not much of natural resources as big as she is. Afghanistan has for more natural resources than India. What India dose they bring up extraordinary students as populated as they are. India send them around the world and use their students for future and benefit of India in all sectors of their country.

Today we are facing English language in every profession we choose. There is more countries that communicate in English around the world than native English spoken are so what we must do we have to teach all the subjects in English language in all of our Schools colleges and universities and so on the reason I am writing this we have to be able to communicate with outside world and do business with for the prosperity of our nation. If we cannot communicate with them how we can understand each other. Of course our own beautiful languages of Pashtu Dari Farsi Tajik is there as well. That will be also a subject to learn them properly and we practice it at home with families loved ones and friends so forth.

Now I like to talk about our brain it has been said by money respected medical researchers in the world and there researches shows that we only use five percent of our brain. Can you believe this any normal human being are using only five percent of his or her brain. see god the merciful give us that kind of a gift if we go on and use six or seven percent of our brain what we can do in a way god the merciful give us unlimited power for each one of us to use it for good of our nation and the world

You see how kind god is to us but when we use that smarts to do evil things how disappointed god must get. The history shows good always prevails over evil well never when because god is not in their side. God says when you walk I am beside you at all-time never be afraid of anything I am with you.

Now I like to talk a bit about the political parties or (hezbs) in Afghanistan we have enough experiences with them from 1979. The communist party's came to power after the coup and fall of sardar Muhammad Dahood who was murdered with his entire family peace up on his soul all of these Communist's political party in the name of khalk and parcham. The very first thing they did they sold our country to Russians and the jihad started. As you all know we lost in the war with Russians two million men and women far better than you and I and there are so money people walking around Afghanistan without limbs due to their Russians land mines. After the civil war started in the name of seven or eight Different Political parties and all of them did not cooperate with each other or anybody one at all these war lords was worse than all of them.

They wanted no comfort for Afghanistan or its people. They wanted power for themselves and for themselves only what kind of result we have gotten from that only the total destructions of Afghanistan after fighting each other for years. So bad for so long Afghanistan went back to Stone Age as result. Nothing left anymore and all of these political parties gotten weak from fighting their own brothers and finally a group came from Pakistan in the name of Taliban; backed by ISI of Pakistan and they occupied our beloved country in matter of days. What they have done was the crime of century. There is no place for me to say anything for what they have done?

You have seen the horror they have created the world was amazed by these barbarians. Now with help of US and NATO has we gotten the structure of Afghanistan back the cooperation of Afghan people from south to north and from east to west each one of us must feel responsible what responsible means it means to be able to respond just a bet of look out for the enemy and report when they see something suspicious with this age of cellular phones. We must have a short memorized Police Number to be able to contact the police and report the situation in matter of minutes. If it is out of Police hands they will contact the governor of that province and he or she will involve the army and so forth. That's how we could save ourselves and our neighborhood for that matter.

Most of us question the government. So what kind of help I am going to receive from them. Let's think different for a while. Let's change your way of thinking—brain storm it and keep on brain storming it until you reach a positive conclusion so you will have whatever you want as westerners says if there is will there is way. Let's go with it keep on thinking the way you do and might be strange push you self to the (might) it is time for you to help the area you live in bring changes for better. Surprise the people of that province the short cuts and smart moves over and over again until the people of your province admire you and follow you for the goods that you are doing and offer help to the government. How is that for a change . . .

President Karzai have done a lot for our Country that was not easy to held all those meetings around the world and trying to put things in prospective somehow again while his life is in danger and any moment could be in to target of a terrorist which they tried four or five times. They shot at him and wanted to take his life mercilessly. He survived it and it is not easy to go around in Afghanistan and make speeches. He put his life on the line of fire to make sorting out of nothing what do us have there is nothing stones and large mountains where the enemy can hide and could be very difficult for anyone to go and look all over those huge mountains and fight them that in country are made for wars like this to hide and seek and terror that's about it.

Afghan did not say thank you to president karri for what you have done for us. The only thought in Afghans mind is what did he do for me and my Family reminds me of the famous speech of president John F. Kennedy again as he said ask not what your Country can do for you but ask what you can do for your country.

Really think of these words for a moment please if you want to have a better future. If each family cleans front of their house the wall street would be clean. Always love one in other. Respect each other. Live the life whatever it is make the best out of it I know we are poor nation but some day it will change for the better. I assure you if we bother to do only good we have to be optimistic and hardworking individuals who are hopeful and better tomorrow never lose hope. That hope is that keep us alive and well may be for most of you don't know I was an abused child. My own mother did things to me; you don't want to do to your worst enemy what kept me alive. That hope and the resilient that each child or young man has. You might think what kind of family my mother came from. Some of you who know her you know I am telling the truth.

She came from the royal family of Afghanistan from both sides. Father side and mother side she was not as educated or maybe she had this dieses called sadism. Life is a struggle. Fight it like you are in a Boxing Ring; fighting someone very strong and tough after all we are Afghans.

Now we must as a one nation must work together in smart way to reach our goals just like the soccer game. We must pass for each other at any giving moment we can't be selfish if we have this negative feeling only me or my province we cannot win ever give each other a chance. Don't think what is in it for me. Be generous, give away to each other with kindness after all how long we will live and when we pass on what we will take with our self's only a piece of white cloth that's all, but our souls will be rich. And in state of comfort and joy for what good I have done and left behind basically that is our reward and treasure after life.

Rummy was an afghan men who was an incredible poet philosopher of his time he went to exile to Turkey. The afghan government of that time thought he was crazy or trouble maker he turned out to be one of the best poet and philosophers and educators ever. His books has been translated to so many languages in the world. Rummy say's whatever stream of feelings and blood runs in your body. I feel it here in me.

So miss understanding conflicts. Prejudice is going on around and runs like a river but the only way to resolve it through studies, research, reading and learning until the time you cannot see or hear no more. Most of the day we think we are thinking, but that is not the case what we are doing is we are judging others, and that is not only solving any issues that we might have it makes our problems only worse.

Then what it is. Our life will be in general difficult to live with ourselves and others.

Dear Afghans we are talking about civilization never came to any modern country overnight. First of all let's find out how we can reach it always starts with small businesses from candy stores all the way how to make airplanes. Each business started from one store to two stores as they expand the business the owner of the businesses with its staff are asking how to serve the people better. What the people prefer the most how we can make the customers happier with the prices looking out for comfort of people that's how the small stores changes to small businesses.

And after that to corporations yes ladies and gentlemen cooperation's means that business has more than 500 employees and hiring people to work, and getting a name for itself people trusted that company they always get paid on time and that company may provide its staff with medical Insurance and the employees are and after certain age they have a retirement plan, and that's how these cooperation's helps the government and the government's job gets easier by the day if sometimes, god forbid if these Companies gets in some sort of financial problems that's when government certainly will help and gets that company out of trouble.

The aim of modern countries are very different they always think of at least two hundred years to the future for example America always has deals with OPIC or oil petrol incorporated to buy there gas and oil from Arab emeritus. America has reserved oil for at least two hundred years to use but they don't they buy the OPIC oil first; I think you got the picture.

Now we are facing a very difficult task for this afghan generation and the next in order to get our self's together the reason I am writing this book because I know Afghans we are pure people we are not some weasel manipulative knifing people, we lost so money people and we are all over bloody because of our good hearts and simplicity don't ever trust no one again people are dirty you know it and I know it don't let that land to be demolished again with tears in my eyes I am asking you "Don't, for god sake don't!"

In America here where I live Virginia for the past twenty years are so every weekend there is a funeral to go to Afghans are dying because they don't have tomorrow to look forward to and you back home are thinking what the lucky Afghans they live in America. Please don't ever think that way again we are not South Americans we are Afghans.

Not so long ago Japan as you all know is an island surrounded by sea and has been there to help afghan people for a long time. Not long ago a severe tsunami hit that nation so bad the all country almost went under the water. The family's there couldn't find even their personal belongings there. Five atomic reactors has been damaged the all world got scared what would happen if they explode. They did not even asked their neighbors for help. They give the nation the time by when everything we lost comes back in normal again no body heard that brave nation even complaining about it they did what they had to do to put everything in order again. We should learn from them we have to show resilience as the great scientist of century Albert inciting put it I want to know what the god thinks like everything else are (details) think about it what he said for a moment.

After the professionalization of natural science during the nineteenth century, though it was common for physicists to seek support in their religious belief or lack of belief in a transcendent god few reported turning to scientific study primarily out of religious motivations as had been the case during the seventeenth, and early eighteenth centuries one remarkable exception was Albert Einstein for who self-reported religious reasons played a major role in both motivations of his own scientific work and his interpretations of the scientific work of others since his views or views very much like his have strongly influenced the attitudes of many important very much like his have strongly influenced the attitudes of many important theoretical physistes, and cosmologists well into the late Twentieth century the dessert special attention.

Einstein's religion was in no sense based on the notion of the personal god or orthodox who demanded obedience and punished disobedience I cannot conceive of a god who rewards, and punishes his creatures he wrote do not can me nor would I want to conceive of an individual that survives his physical death let feeble souls from fear or absurd egoism cherish such thoughts, Einstein after a brief period of orthodoxy commit to what he later identified as entirely impersonal and entirely rational god a firm belief a belief bound up with deep feelings in a superior mind that reveals itself in the world of experience represents my conception of god objective aspect of god led him to the unshakable belief that the universe had a real existence independent of all observers and that it had to be totally causal and deterministic.

More over cause god was completely rational Einstein was convinced throughout his life that a complete. Understanding of the natural world must oppose both positivist assertions that science could be nothing. But the systematized record of our sensations, and all causal and statistical interpretations of quantum mechanics the search for some kind of grand unified theory or theories of everything based on a conviction that physics must ultimately be not only consistent with our sensory experiences, but also logically inevitable, and faceable of account in from everything including the reason for the origin of the universe continuing or everything including the reason for the origin of the universe continuing for issues among physicists oat the beginning of the twenty first century.

These logics we are creating for our world they are all make sense, but when it comes to human, you might say why sultan masoud talks about a famous scientist the reason for that is, his philosophy in our modern World and explaining everything in detail to me is vital to put it on the paper because what he shows us they are not only interesting it's important because he was a famous physicist people will believe him for more than me as an unknown person.

As every government is responsible for their Ute it is very sad to see so money afghan children I saw today November/ 20/ 2012 the young children washing tires of vehicles in our capital Kabul instate of being in school. They look like to be great students, forced to wash tires at age of my own son instead of being in school. What is wrong with this picture where is the governor to make some kind of arrangements to provide their family's with some kind of help, and have these incent children go to school as soon as possible before it's late what you try to do make a criminal out that children and Afghan government will has to pay for it later in future. Please take this seriously we need to see a fluctuation soon in this very important issue looking at it is unbearable to me each one of them needs to be managed the governor staff must take them personally, and show them their schools and to be signed in and their school Principal must report to governor s staff office regularly they show up on time in their class rooms so they don't waste a day washing those tiers.

A mind is a trouble think to waste, all of human brains are the same size and what shape only Afghans are better looking. Genius can come out of it any minute depends of what they are concentrating about when the society not allowing a young man to concentrate on something so in future of that nation use him or gets its benefit to bring about intellect, and make life easier for the citizen of that nation that will not be tangible on concentrating washing those tires. A young man majoring in physics by name of Albert Einstein as he was not washing tires that day he was setting in his class room alone he looks at the clock of his class room, moving as he looks deeper in to that clock he looks at the motion of the clock. He gets more curious he looks at the clock more and more he realizes there at that time the faster you travel the more time slows, but a think or a person moving at a slower speed experiences time differently than a person a speed of light, and comes to a conclusion to write the theory called theory of relativity. Newton theory of gravitation was soon accepted without question of his special theory of Relativity in 1905 in his Several Theory of relativity in 1915 hire is an example of through experiment in Special Relativity first showed that Newton law of gravitation was also only approximately correct.

Breaking down in the presence of very strong gravities in field we shall consider relativity in more details later here we only we summarize the differences between Newton theories of gravitation implied by general theory of relativity prediction as long as the strength of the gravitation field is weak which is our usual experience however there are crucial predictions where the two theories diverge and this can be tested with careful experiments the General theory of relativity predicts light coming from a strong gradational field should have its wave Length shifted to larger values what astronomers call a red shift again cents to Newton Theory once again detailed observations indicates such a red shift and that is magnitude is correctly given to be Einstein's Theory, the reason I have mentioned these scientific theories trying to point out how when you allow a young mind to study and research can accomplish so much not only for their own country, but for the world as well.

Our great religion Islam is the latest a sacred our god and our prophet wants it to be intact. Wants to be admired around the world. Islam is not only for Muslims it is for all intelligent people who has a question, and needs an answer. So open our holy book and find the answer our prophet. Peace up on him, he wanted that our religion to be respected in great manners that's why every Muslim is so proud.

Of intellect of our holy religion he wants us to be humble of it, and share it with the world in very much peaceful manner intellectually and professionally, and we must obey that and be humble and follow our peaceful religion to look at history all of the wisdom in human history has come from east to west. Following our religion all of great thinkers and educators of Islam provide the west, with power of intellects and they have thought the westerners so many way, and philosophy of life so they can improve them as well, but somehow time and circumstances made us look a bit weak that doesn't mean. We were nobody, we were the masters of the world and the history shows that over, and over but we need to be humble about it we need to share with them not in anger not in any manner, but with class dignity and the fashion as possible so they don't get confused about our great greatest of all religions.

The Ultimate Islam, Muslims name their child after our the greatest prophet I never heard in western Country's some one name their child after their prophet Jesus but I cannot common on that more because I am not a scholar so we have to be humble, and be good to any other religion has there prophet name is in our holy book Koran being kind is the only way and solution for the future of our humanity every moment of Muslim countries is about religion who doesn't say god every moment, and who is not asking help from their profits who is not feeling god in themselves for a split of a second who you tell me, what they are doing they are degrading our religion, and have you ever heard from other countries about their profits every second we need to learn, and handstand Islam, and practice every word that is in Koran, but not scream on the streets in the name of that great religion when angels appeared on the mountain where the prophet Mohammed peace up on him was mediating in the form of an Angel and asked our profit read Mohammed peace up on him ha got secured because he was a human and thirty chapter of Koran was completed they called the religion Islam it means peace and absolute surrendering to god all mighty completely any one read the Koran and they hander stood and said that the Koran cannot be retina by human it has to be from God they all accepted the religion and Mohammed peace up on him as the messenger of the god he did have his straggles like any other massagers of the god Islam did not come overnight our profit peace up on him had deal with some of those who was questioning him like Mhoya with the strong army of almost two thousand he was saying to our profit may be you are a philosopher or a genus but we cannot accept you as the massager of the god we want see your magic's like any other messengers of the god Mohamed responded my magic is my book Koran if you are questioning me I have no choice, but to fight you and people came and said you holiness to messenger of god we only have Three hundred men most of them are yang has no training in fighting and the others are old men we possibly cannot win with the enemy Mohammed peace up on him responded then why I am the massager of god get ready we are going to war it doesn't matter how strong they are just get ready we are going to War with moyah in the next few days Mohammed peace up on He was up front and they went to war with the strongest army of that time moyah. In a matter of days Mohamed peace up on him demolished the enemy and prevailed.

As they traveled all over The Middle East and Europe as they introduced religion of Islam not with war or force of any kind they represent the holly book Koran and the massager of the god and they have treated people with respect and kindness even in Europe profit has said anyone who is Christians who goes to churches we will love them like our brother and sisters or Jewish men and women who goes to syngag we will respect them and treat them like our brothers.

We love them as our brothers and sisters it is in our holly book Koran if we make friends with other religion's and go have dinner with them that is goodness and we as Muslims is highly recommended and get to know each other and learn from each other with kindness and respect our book Koran is a peace full book how much they have showed respect to Christ peace up on him and how much of a respect for profit Abraham peace up on him and all other messengers from god to the earth for the people and love them as your brothers and sisters.

Yes ladies and gentle man we shall not allow anyone to highjack our religion and miss use it for their own political purposes our religion is our religion and it will be with us until we die and go to Other Side. I talked so much about religion I feel like some old religions sculler or something I want to go out and play now, and be a kid as I am.

Any country which is beginning to go towards civilization must start with a logical strong, and great Constitution law a constitution law that everyone agrees with it, and that should stay for long time so people follow, and respect that.

Not long ago I have sued Russians in United Nations as the president of Russia Mr. Putin was coming to pay a visit here in Washington D.C. with US president; for occupation of Afghanistan, and there atrocity's to our nation the Russians refused to pay a dime for reconstruction of Afghanistan and General Secretary of United Nations couldn't do anything about it they have international lawyers and lots of power in Newark to enforce the law but I don't know may be that was a big task at this time. Or maybe the secretary Of United Nations Mr. Ban KY moon was busy with other things they were saying something about former secretary of UN Mr. Kofi Annan that he was a bit decaffeinated but anyways we do have to have allots of respect for UN they are working hard and they are dealing with the all world's problems after all the poor nation like us that's all we have to look up to and asking for our writs that is almost our only hope.

We are coming back to our domestic solution's again we have to work with enthusiasms and kindness to reach our goals I hear about corruptions in our land I have to Say for everything there a reason I am sure no one will do such thing if they receive a good decent salary so there Income would take care of his family and I saw in in the news a solder that was near the border fighting. He was complaining that he did not receive his salary for almost two months now how sad that can be that man is putting his life under fire and we don't bother to send his salary to him on time that is almost tragic to me than how we possibly keep the Afghans interested in their jobs writing about modernization of Afghanistan if we don't keep people happy with the salary they receive as well as promotions and a nice life style they will not stay home they may be want to go to the Arab Emeritus so for kind of work they are doing be appreciated and get paid on time, people are you with me.

This is very important please keep them, and their families save and happy as happy they can get. The investments Afghans are making for example in dub, and other neighbor countries at this time and the financial situation Afghanistan is a crime, the department of treasury must not allow any Afghans to take a dime out Afghanistan we have to have money circulate in Afghanistan like the blood in the body, having said that as we all know the Afghani has no value every one dealing with dollar's and Afghani has lost value that needs to be fixed have the rent of the house that expansive did any leaders of that country taught how this poor afghan nation will possibly can pay for the rent of an Apartment or House food clothing and medication this is another kind of torture for Afghans called inflation or financial atrocities we need to fix that once for all.

The concentration of afghan government must not only be on the capital, Kabul but to pay attention on other provinces to build and improve the people lives as soon as possible obviously every one approaching Kabul there is no space, and thinks are getting more expensive and difficult by the day there.

By the way why Afghan governments throughout the history has been concentrating on Kabul only there other 28 provinces to think about and take care of; we must change that in western world other Cities and states are more beautiful, and more prospers than there capital is. There are lots of jobs in America and in Europe today through software computers telephone services internet technicians called networking that afghan qualified yang men and women who knows English can do now, India is doing it as we speak and they get paid very well.

In the old days there was only some English newspapers, and some movies to there wasn't even television when I was in Kabul now with this modern technology's I pod phones smart phones, and especially internet that you not only can read it you can also see for yourself any questions you might have there is an answer for it that is not invented for noting we all should use it from modern haircuts to dresses all kinds of fashion home designs from dental information to anything you want is in the tip of your fingers why we don't use it, and learn it.

I like to talk about the study's specially young generation to day mostly what we need is architectures for the road, and houses big hospitals memorials statues bridges men and women should think of architecture when you build a building designs it, and calculates the all systems in that building and get to finish it and that building or bridge will stay forever, and your name is on it who designing it and that is a memory for generations to come and admire your work, and appreciate it takes a look at your picture who build it who was that women or men now that is an accomplishment to respect for very long time.

I ask specially the government to be appreciative of it, and all of lady's get to thank that architecture. We need to show our respect and how great full we are as an afghans who has tried to make our nation look good, and bring comfortable facility's and we enjoy looking at that buildings or bridges or that structure with pride, and joy and it needs to be televised.

When I was eleven years old before we left to another country I remember the way of constriction we usually use very much of heavy material to build a building like heavy stones and heavy breaks makes the construction or building almost back breaking In America the construction workers who build houses I have seen them they use mostly woods, and the stuff they use to build a building are very light of course they do use the structures with the iron somehow they are building a two story beautiful building in matter of months I know they have the tools, but they are doing it so smart with some kind of knowledge and technology that it is Amazing how fast they build it since Americans is there now we should invite one of their constructions Companies to come in Kabul and show how the system works as they say if you give a fish for a person you feed them for a day, but if you teach him how to fish you feed them for a life time.

Art of the possible: a frequent definition of politics stressing the need for compromise asking not what must be done but what can be done. Political figures under fire for falling short of attaining lofty goals promised in campaigns often fall back on the phrase the art of possible as a useful defense. It emphasizes practical nature of political rule with its built-in checks and balances.

Ironically the source is rarely quoted the chancellor of defined politics as the doctrine of possible the attainable . . . the art of the next best a master of the art of the possible in politics. Frequently in life I have had to settle for progress short of perfection. I have done so because of cynics I believe that half a loaf is better than none. But my acceptance has always been conditioned upon the premise that the half-loaf is a step toward the full-loaf—and that if I go on working the day of the full loaf will come.

We do not need politics in that poor nation now we need reformation as I said as united we stand as divided we fall. As we all know we Afghans have anger issues it is not just now it has been there for very long time will I hander stand when someone wants to occupied your country or wants to hart your family or try to personally you have very written to be angry and respond to that I don't know where this anger is coming from, but it is in us we have to do something about that some people don't know are proud of that somehow to me anger is the most hart full think ever in a society if especially when that nation is going towards reformation when you do any think in state of mind that you are angry or upset you never can accomplish that task Somehow and you block others going towards improvement I remember when I was at third grad in Kabul my math teacher she was angry most of the time she was wearing a light blue color uniform when I didn't know the answer she would of hit me with stick or pulling my hair smacking me somehow I kind of lost interest in math and that issue never been resolved what an important subject to thank god for calculators and excel.

One other thing comes to mind as we all know the marriages in Afghanistan true history has been mostly between cousins or first cousins I might say that is absolutely banded in most of other nations because the science and medical research shows that when a men and a women has a chilled from the same group of the blood there is going to be a lots of medical issues in that child as he or she is growing up they are going to face complications in that chilled emotionally physically or it will be anger Issues this Problem has been dominated our nation because the families are the same so they feel very much comfortable with that marriages while the future of that Nation is at jeopardy this has to stop once for all it should be in our law books.

The money that is coming home from other nations who helps if we don't use the money to build factory's with it not in Kabul may be in other provinces try to make our own cloth, and basically machines that we can use for agricultures and tailoring equipment's medical supply's cranes for constrictions of buildings tractor for essffalts of streets bringing educational programs to television useful commercials for people specially building schools like we know now most of students are able to go to schools not only structure of schools but new tables chair boards, and hiring educators from around the world to write new text books for all levels from first grad to universities and on up to date With education of today's world all the curriculums again it has to be thought in English language all levels if we don't have the teachers to instruct we have to ask other nations to come and teach our schools colleges and universities I am sure there government will pay them to come in Afghanistan and teach for free until our own instructors are trained and qualified to replace the instructors who came from other nations to help teaching this is a very serious task it has to be implemented it is about the future and civilization of Afghanistan.

Sometimes I watch afghan television here in US, there is a chubby short man name Mr. Bay at gives people oil corn basically food supplies the people who receive the supplies that embarrass them they must distributes the food in some sort of respectable fashion in to a in a big buildings they must use computers and people should have identification based on that so the people Receive their weekly or monthly food distribution on time until we get our selves together and reformation comes to a point that there is job for everyone and retirement plans takes place.

You must take pride at any level of job you are responsible for and get to be the best at it when you see a construction worker look at them like how proud of him you are, and respect him job is a job it doesn't matter what it is be proud of it and enjoy doing it you know what is the worst job is high level jobs like being the president of the country or to be a minister or so on because they are under fire of press and they have the biggest responsibilities they have to answer for everything and people judge them every day and make them responsible for thinks they never know if that even existed, and being under spot lights twenty four hours is not an easy task again we have to make sure of our constitution law which is the most important in our daily lives to be are ten in a profound great detailed law so we all are touched by it, and feel it in our veins so we shall obey it and practice it in our daily lives, and as I see and hear every twenty person has a political parity in the name of this and in the name of that that is not only make us look miss lead and misunderstood it degrades the value of our nation.

One constatituation one flag (the Islamic republic of Afghanistan) as we look at it with pride and we firmly stand up, and as tears comes rolling on our cheeks we salute that holly flag of ours, and be great full for the land of ours as we walk on it, and say to ourselves it's mine I am not a forghner. As you read this book you might say ho . . . sultan masoud wants to be the father of our country, no I am Yang I go around, and laugh and make others laugh like a kid I enjoy listing to music and same time I prefer being alone more than anything, anyways so much about me.

We must aim high put our standards in quality to never parish again first start with our self's than our family's we shouldn't always make an excuse the economy what is money after all that can buy certain things only it is being printed in some machine don't let ever think because you don't have money you are nobody. You are that human who starts the machine the money to be printed that piece of paper we call it money and I am not saying it is not important it is that's why every on struggling breaks sweat and blood to make it. I am not naïve, but our Values comes first may be we don't have allots of cloths to where but whatever we have we washed it clean; ware it with style and confidence that will make you look good and make me look good as well.

I want to talk about Americans it is not easy to hander stand them for long time but Americans or America has been made of emigrants for past four hundred years from all walks of life they have crossed the ocean with ships to this big island that looked like paradise in nature mostly from I would say poor families they started here almost with noting only four generations or four fathers with hard work honesty Compassion Cooperation to each other and some basic civil wars between the states. Later on all became united that's why they call it United States each state is very much big for example state of Texas in the east coast is exactly about the size of Afghanistan there was war with Great Brittan until America had their independence from great Brittan they also have celebration and Fire Works on the Fourth of July each year they are proud strong people also they managed to be the most beautiful country in the world now they call them the super power and they are indeed powerful but they are kind, and have been around the world to help and solve lots of issues for past sixty years or so.

The world needs America today there always some kind of incidents domestically or in war we never can Judge, and generalize a country with it now if Americans are in Afghanistan they just try to help that's all and this good men and women in uniform with good hearts and clean ambitions they have for us we need to treat them with kindness and show our gratitude to them for losing some of their men if they pull out now our lives would be like eleven years ago dealing with Taliban they are firing rockets at our country as we speak we have nothing you know it, and I know it Afghan man is out of energy and we cannot fight now like 1980's we are injured therefore we need to think wisely how important America is to us.

You might ask what this name America they call came from, long ago in South America at that time North America was not established much there was a Spanish man in south and he was a Mayer in some town up there they say he was a good fair man people liked him for what he has been doing for that particular town by the name of AMERCO so after his pass they named the north and south after him now they pronounce it America.

All of this great country's based on democracy first of all what this word democracy means it's is an Italian word it means for People or justice for all in our chamber of afghan congress we should always think different we argue and get the majority vote in a peace full manner our thoughts should be for each other like maybe I don't agree with a word that you are saying but I would give my life for you that you will be able to say what you have in mind.

Another issue for our young generations who was born in west if they are not fluent in Pashtu language or Dari or Farsi or tank we should not judge them by it if even speak only English or French or German it doesn't mean that they have less feeling for his or her country than us may be they have for more feeling for Afghanistan as you know they are western educated with that young energy and spontaneous urge that they have to help rebuilt the nation we must respect them and listen to their advices as professional they are most family spend lots of money for their children to get the proper education and come home and help we do have here 'young man and women to come not only to just help but shake up our nation for biter we must be very much appreciative of them and respect them and protect them and treat them like our own family members for our better tomorrow.

They say here between an ordinary and extraordinary is just a little bit that needs discipline whatever outside home that we waiting for we should fallow the rolls if we are waiting to get a ticket to go to movies we must make lines naturally the early person should receive hers or his ticket first and it goes on the next Person we should adjust our selves for better reforms one other very important issue Afghans all don't pay attention where they are if we are in class room we have to be in class room emotionally 100% or any other think just think of the situation you are at until you resolve it or completed it successfully than you go to the next project the next project to Deal with one think at the time that's how westerners are improving by daily basis.

The basic reformations is that makes the country civilized in everyday life improvements let's think of children who goes to school every day— if the school is a bit far—how they get to school by walking or to take public bus or taxi cab how they can be on time in their classes we have to have special school busses for each school so the school bus picks up from the area each student and drops them back to their homes with a security guard and safety that can be a peace of mind for their parents as well as students and school staff and directors. We have to think of our own area we are living at and make sure that sector is safe if we see any danger or something suspicions with this age of cellar phone we must report it to local police as soon as we can.

Life dose have disappointments there is a book rated by the great American writer among way later on the holly wood made a movie based on that book staring Spenser tressy he was a fisher man with the small Ship that he had living around the ocean everyone saw that the huge wale around that ocean Spencer Trecy decided to couch that wale; he waited few days and nights to catch that wale as he was sleeping one night he felt his ship is unusually moving he woke up looked at those ropes and he saw that wale that is caught by him and started working and pulls the wale to himself as the rain is pouring hard and the wind is blowing forcefully there is a raging storm his ship is getting unbalanced and water of the sea splashes to his Ship and inside as well he is all by himself and keeps on puling the Wale his hands is bloody as the wale is bleeding in the ocean too all the Sharks and other sea Species attacks that wale and start eating her and the wale forcing in other direction the fisher men Is Personal with that Wale now he keeps on talking to her as the night is about to become Duane and his hands are bleeding and he is existed when he finally pulls the wale to his ship he sees there is only Bones left of her and looks at her and says . . . my poor fish . . . and passes out.

Think to help the brain or a group of advisors; or specifically or a research organization developing plans and projects for government and defense connect industries the phrase enjoyed a brief period as substitute for brain trust as politicians turned to colleagues for task and new approaches to solving new and old problems this meaning was surprised with the emergence of the social science can exercise and Socialize in pleasant surroundings while doing profound research and planning on government assignments.

Scientists to work in civilians surroundings but wanted to keep their brain power available to the military establishment. Observers impressed with high level intellectual atmosphere. The work of thinking is often to the work done by universities and industrial research and development departments and management Consultants although the term is used arbitrarily the think have one thing is common all are groups of men and women with impressive credentials who conduct interdisciplinary research.

In politics while I hate the term politics as they say nobody knows what is in mixture in politics or in sausages anyways I must go on in politics as well as science the nassasaty for solitude and time to figure out plans and programs in midst of hectic complains is always a problem.

Talk about the treatment of women in Afghanistan when this is going to stop; forcefully orange marriages you are making life hell for them without women no one can possibly can come to this world how could you disrespect them so much—this is getting really out of control—we need to stop that once for all, you are killing their souls they don't know how to talk or dress or express themselves anymore the media around the world shows the crimes being committed to women in our country it is shamefully embarrassing slashing them in middle of the circles of people you know how damaging this can be to their confidence, the people who knows me they know I can be bad I would bomb you so bad there will be hard for grasses to grow in that area again please stops it.

There was a profit of god was walking by looking over and sees there is a crowd is gathered he comes closer that all these men Wants to Stone that women who is sitting in the middle he asks why the men answers she committed some Kind of crime the profit of god say' to them will ok go head stone her, but I want the very first person who throws the stone should be the one who never did any sin in his life time all of them looked at each other and dropped the Stones, and went back about their business the profit took her back to her house after words she became a holly woman.

I personally invite the men and women who took the advantage of occupation of Russians and made it an excuse to get out of the country without feeling any responsibility's or remorse to their country by using the name and blood of true men, and women who fought Russians coming to west and enjoys the life here or there as refugees now some of them I know personally who became milliners here they have all Kinds of Businesses clinics, and so on here in America and in Europe never looked back just used the name of that bloody country to get somewhere somehow, and sang songs and said poems about it for just an hour in a party to have a good time, and they know their children are in safety and has a good future while the country is bleeding and, we are looking at only some entertainment or some ting we enjoy here in west and basically in our core we are ashamed of it, and we see in our own eyes and we keep on try to ignore it and we say NATO is there because life is good here aren't we and we should be ashamed of our self's or maybe I am saying that because my dad is not well and I am getting older and can't party like I used to, any ways I must go on with this book.

Today in the globe the economy and finance is playing a major role and it is dominating the world our neighbor china has improved its economy so great that they are competing with United States of America for a Communist nation a decade ago it was unthinkable, but now they are emerging to be another super Power in the world not too far away from us just a neighbor you might ask how they did it the answer to that is simple by working hard discipline and thinking maturely they are making products in numerous amount of factory's and they sell it in half price or less to the world and there product is not is that bad people with financial situation will buy their products now they even came to America opened stores called wall mart for less than half price they buy their products why not they are all over the place and they don't care the pollution they cause that it comes to our country from there factory's the only think they have is factories and population there is no life or style just making goods and sales those to the world that's in other way of doing business regardless of any body make yours self-stronger how about that lets learn from them too wye not they put their people to Work to make goods, and they keep it quiet one of their mature thinking was giving 80 Years China asked to get the Keys back from England and England gave them the honking now It is money making state, and as beautiful as it became it is money making machine for china and this is called mature thinking. The world rapidly is getting smaller because of the technology we have to adapt our self's as well in Order to survive and not being called one of the poorest nations in the world that needs cooperation with blue eyes people and any one ells who wants to do business with us our country is created by Diversity like north and south let's cleans our hearts not being revengeful so much they say if you want Revenge—you need to dig two graves—one for yourself and one for that let us not be afraid of them person who you want to get Revenge from peace at any price a slogan formerly used in earnest now an attack phrase on those considered appeasers the idea of a price to be paid for peace probably stemmed from the price for Liberty. Eternal vigilance is the price of liberty is the quotation developed Afghanistan's prosperity at any Price safety comes first instead the love of soft living and to get rich quick by corruption feeling guilty and to pay the price for peace is a Quotation with the substitution of life for living at the end.

Typical use of the wind metaphor in modern times was by Indian Prime Minister Jawaharlal Nehru; in 1947; the masses are awake and they demand their heritage. Strong winds are blowing all over Asia. Let us not be afraid of them but rather welcome them for only with their help can we built the new Asia of our dreams on that note we Afghans have no choice but get involved without side world and see what can we do to make a better tomorrow for Afghanistan I know the bullets are crossing our head we have to duck and play smart to live and fight another day you may be ask when this unfortunate life and misery will be over let's be hopeful we came a long way from eleven years ago it's better than noting we have to read those books coming from all over the globe—one page at time handstand it—and practice it people are writing novels fiction and story's which is just for wasting time we have no time for that we have to read only nonfiction books on facts not lies there will be some day when thinks are better and we having good incomes and Afghanistan is built and it's safe so we can drive our family In each Season in a province that they can have a good time for a weekend.

To establish growth and economy for the future we have to work with people in each province in the Nation and its people knows what they need for the people who has good ideas for businesses there the Government must work with them by giving them loans so they can open their business and grow their Business and hiring people in that province and as soon as their business are established they should pay back the loan with a little interest to the government this way we have people employed people gets back there money even more and the government make people responsible for themselves in each sector of the country that's how we can get out of poverty and Afghanistan can put their first steps toward civilization and we have to talk brief move fast dress light shave we don't have to wear our custom very day we should live it for celebrations so proudly so we can say I am a proud afghan and this is my custom for that holiday.

We all respect our elders and they need to have retirement plans after certain age that way we really respected them in the same token we need to respect our very yang for more than the elders any one can take care of them gets to be 100 years old that comes naturally but our yang needs more respect that's when they develop their personality and manners we have to answer very smart and carefully I saw a five year old baby in television asks her mother an impossible question she asks Mom dose god has feet as strange that Sounds we have to be prepared for their questions, and respond in very intelligent way each child when they born they are genus as they grow up when they see something is wrong that's the time the child loses his or her concentration thinks more about why is that whatever they look at it is recorded in their minds forever we should not even allow our self's to argue front of a Child because we put their future in jeopardy especially at this time so we call Terrorism is Persuasion by fear the and intimidation of society by small group using as its weapons that society's repugnance at the murder of innocent's.

Terrorism may have originated with for personal reasons it can be in country or someone power full abusing his or her power so that system unrespectable violence to coerce others into obedience or in modern times to trigger such official Repression as to encourage revolution in the names of secrets employing terrorism have become synonyms for violence or Irrationality my screaming heart says home became a cage where is the forest to gather with loins my village is burning where is a bit of rain?

As I put the good and bad of life together where mathmation to divide that is maybe it is easy for me to make suggestions writing this book, but I believe in looking forward, and never look back no matter how much of pain we carry in our hearts we have no choice, but to move on we even have a bit of chemical in our brain not to feel so much of reality they call it resilient that's how we get to continue living but we need to play the game of life smart I know the fears sound of bombs and guns were not allow us to read a book through the years while the jewel and crowns of nation has been killed one by one they were not here to defend us but I believe in peace will come and we will prevail somehow as Afghans are Famous for their good looks hope fully we see in future a good looking country as well in so money way's we got hurt by our self's or others playing with us and there were days our king and president was driving while there left elbow was out of the window without a single security guard people honored each other we need to bring that respect for each other back and live without any fear that needs work cooperation of the people and most of all our scullers needs to talk to people about kindness and the meaning of it most of you might say he is a good writer what is that mean I did not waste any of my Time I studied researched learned while working and having a fun at the same time now I am older and it is payback time for me. America was good to me they are simple kind people one thing you learn here is not to lie and that is important for each of us.

Negativism it's is a word that makes people to be pessimistic when you are pessimistic that is contest and that will bring a country down at any level in contrary optimistic is the opposed and we need to be optimistic at anything when you are that you are happy and that is contest as well that's where country is going towards prosperity we should never forget that if we don't work with each other and make each other look good we will not achieve anything opposed of it is division and we saw that through the years how that are going to work out for us.

Afghans our goal should not be just surviving that way of thinking weakening us more we must completely erase that way of thinking out of our minds we must imaging we are in World Olympics and we are running for gold and we should never sat ale for only silver medal we need to shake up and show the world we could achieve things they never thought of we could possibly ever.

This is from a famous educator in the west she says if you think you can or you cannot you write both ways think about that for a moment future and civilization of Afghanistan is up your way of thinking if you think you can we well reach that gold if we think we can't we will be still afraid of Pakistanis when we we're making fun of them at 1970s it's up to you when a lion is injured Haines wants attack them and eat them That Is nature of the beast we must put our standards high and play smarter than anyone ever before because it is a revolutionary time of make or break of our nation we can't fight any more. We need to be fox like use our brain Instead defend our self's with tactics and plans in order to overcome the misery we are facing today don't ever think America will leave us alone again they know better now they're not going g to make the same mistake again as Ronald Regan did in 1980s he was the most loved and Charismatic president ever every one love them but the only mistake he made leaving Afghanistan after Soviet Union clasped' in a round table he said we have no need for Afghans any more let's make Friends with Russia and he made an historic speech in Berlin Germany by saying Mr. Grobechove tears down this wall so he did but took the credit for two million afghan bloods without any remorse left them cold without any supervision or a bag of corn what happened after that?

We all know some of scullers used this for their own political agenda Osama bin laden who was squid with Zawahiri who is from Egypt as well start an evil organization in the name of terror around the world in the name of al-Qaida which means base in 1980s from that point on those two never left Afghanistan. They said we can do anything here afghans are hospitable pure Muslims let's use them with money they had they did whatever they wanted and terror are still existing around the world as we speak but one thing ticked off Ronald Reagan was during the afghan Russia war the representative of Mujahedeen had a visit in white house with Ronald Regan during conversation on of mujaadeen leaders asked with thinking why you don't become Muslim mar president he was surprised by this quashing and He didn't like that how can you ask an old man who is Christian, and president of the most powerful country in the world to Change his religion for you as they say you must think before you speak that was damaging for Afghanistan future when high official personalities have meetings with other nation representatives the very first think they do they research about that person what he or she is like and what is there prospective is regarding the issue they are going to talk about even they research personal thinks like what kind of sports they like, and so on we need to be careful.

Low and order is ruling all of civilized nations with today's technology everyone is feeling safe and sound the very first think we should do use the today's technology from the western countries so our police can respond to people in matter of minutes if they find them self's in situation that cannot protect them self's and they feel they are in danger; we must create a very strong police force so people can concentrate on their everyday lives without the fear because when there is fear that will disable a Country regardless.

You must always trust the unknown because unknown has no personal problems with you why god give us friends that are his way of apologizing to us for our immediate families. We should demand for a constructive reading of our voice to be hart not by garbling and mutilating passages but by reading its context so the meaning of it to be judged by our people and they can use it for improvement of Afghanistan or our nation now that we have our land back we should go through sleepless nights thinking how to protected so we don't have to see those night mares again ever and that should be our number one goal until all of the bloods are washed from the streets so we don't have To see our son and dithers body parts and pick up like we are picking up like some kind of vegetable from gardens it brings tears in my eyes just like yours think about it how human can be so vice's and cruel without any remorse for anybody but them self's may be this is hill and we are in it and that fire of hill is never stops and we feel it over and over again we are decent kind simple people. Why that fire is not going away while others are having a good time around the world we get to live only once where is Justice where is it . . .

When people who wants to be our leaders and they take an oath front of very one this issue seems to be periodically after all these wars the country security conscious and loyalty oaths had a brief vogue. Another form of loyalty oath is often required by a political party of its convention delegates; it is a pledge to abide by the decision of the convention and not to bolt if dissatisfied.

Congress enacted legislation that required confederate sympathizers to take the ironclad oath if they wished to regain their civil rights. Due to the situations in our country yang adults left without education and they might feel uneasy about that I am here to tell you education has nothing to do with anything there is goodness in us as humans and creativity that we can turn around thinks for what our country needs the most write now is Physical Talent to make things built staff with your unlivable might and talent and turn around the country for better the soul in us is everything that is for more useful than any education combined an Holly person who has been reading holly Koran all his or her life can even product the future that is Soul which they came a bit close to god that's what I am saying tolerance is vital as Deepak copra an Indian doctor and philosopher of our time rote about Buddha and how Buddhism came about as we all know the Buddha himself came from a wealthy well know family he wanted to find something didn't know what may be survival without having anything; he went to one of massive forest of India as he kept on try for survival he faced money challenges anger danger and so money other thinks as he was mutating day and night talreding the pain and loneliness suffering and did not lose his patient's by try to be enlightened that means an ordinary human wanted to reach god or get very much close to God as he was walking around in that dangers forest with all those dangers animals like tigers loins and dangers species circling around him none of them tried to hart him or attack him because he was in absolute stage of calmness peace and patient's that none of those dangers animals felt any hostility towards him he pet the lions and tigers just like a small house pet and he was safe with them and he enlighten him self's and trough deep thoughts and handers standing he wrote the book and brought the a new religion called Bodh; as the day he was dying every one gathered around him they asked him who were you—were you a prophet—he said no they asked were you an angel he said no they asked who where you he replied as he was taking his last breath I was simply (awake) . . . and he died.

I have read most of Dr. Chopra's books and his work what a genus he is unlivable at first it is not easy to handstand him he is something ells as he gets together with Dr. Wayne Dyer the American philosopher and they are close friends it is a show to watch once as they got together they were talking about Philosophy of life sometimes they are hummers too Deepak Chopra said I remember everything before I was born or conceived Wayne dyer asked him how Deepak copra answered I remember I went with my father and came back with my mother that's how . . .

Hostility's and not being in peace cusses lots of problems especially now that we have the body of Afghanistan back from enemies by the help of NATO it's shameful for us as they want to train our army teach us the tactic's and help us to be able to defend our country they trust us and give us the weapon for trainings and Such instead of being thank full we shoot the gust who wants to help us securing our country That causes a lots of miss trust for afghan people and we are playing with the future of our Country and the future of our children Afghans around the world especially in America we cannot look at them in the eye any more they say what kind of Culture is this there are more than 2000 American Soldiers lost their lives who had family's dreams for better future there waifs sons and how they feel about us now can't we feel anything for anybody else but our self's—it is not enough for god sakes stop it or you will be Sorry the leaders and army generals try to play games it's like you play a football game and you want to Score for both sides we have seen these kinds of games before there is no room for it anymore; we have to stop these foolish games once for all or ells the World's patients are running out why we can't think about peace for a day we are the ones doesn't want comfort for our Self's and our country let's think about that for a moment.

The only thing I think of is there is a need for something very important pcyclogicaly and that needs to be addressed seriously to Taliban or anyone who doesn't want to put there weapon down whatever you all want can be peacefully resolved just call and request your wishes if you are born in Afghanistan or your parents were born in our country Afghanistan just call and request your wishes the government will Provided for you as they say—ask you shall receive whatever it is that can make you happy your elders or represented can come to the parliament or congress freely and they will be heard and keep a Senate Seats if one of the member of Taliban wants be the president or prime minister there should be no problem with that they can run for presidency there will be debate and afterword's it will be referendum or voting will take place who ever has been chosen by people of Afghanistan will have that position if it is presidency or any other high level positions like governing and so on as long as it is peacefully and for reconstruction so Afghanistan as damaged as it is can step towards prosperity and better future and can see a glams of civilization for a change but if you all come like eleven years ago invite al-Qaida and bring back the terror use football stadium in state of sports and hanging people beating everyone nobody can get out of their house because of fear and that will be not acceptable not only for afghan people but by United Nations and international community's as I talked about in so money word about peaceful thinking that is the only choice our religion means peace and surrendering to Almighty god my goal is to go forward with a plan that can get us out this miss and be watch full gives purpose to the waiting like a cat on a stakeout in front of mouse hole for the enemies of Afghanistan because we have no way to the ocean unfortunately we have make friends with Kashmir pay our taxes for them in order to receive goods by their ocean; this is some ting all neighbors countries around the world provide for each other by getting paid for merchandise coming in Afghanistan true their country that way is a win situation for both of our country's to think of it doesn't matter how long you are going to think about it you will reach one solution and that is cooperation with each other noting lasting noting enduring has ever been born from hatred and prejudice except more hatred and prejudice.

Afghanistan to day needs to shake up each afghan should think as an individual's the he or she is the responsible party not only in side of the country but outside around the world as well it is time for a change each one of us should put Pressure in our heads and bring our blood pressure up to be creative come up with something new it doesn't have to be something extraordinary; I know you all are very proud people doesn't matter something simple do something for Afghanistan instead of nothing yang people specially can come up with something new all the time don't ever think it might me look like a show off the world is a show as it turns around itself they only will be appreciative of it; our government is working for us one president and his cabinet can' no do everything as they say when you go to a country there what you see and what has been build and its beauty that you enjoy looking at that is the Character of its people in other words those buildings big bridges and easy life safety enjoyment there did not grow naturally like trees or nature it happened by the People of that nation and there love respect for that land of theirs educators usually pros wade the youngsters to think out of the box in other words be creative as time goes by and goes by very fast as George cable famous mythologist talks about myth of life as the time we born until the time we die we are circling and circling around and around that's how life begins and ends by the way myth means magical or creative thinking and whatever you think about you become that and always be careful what are you thinking about if you think weak you are weak you think strong you are strong just an example as you have an unlimited ability's the ski is limit and a mind is a trouble think to what we afghans should do move forward reach out turn things around for better in every moment of your life why we should do that we are

Afghans we are unfortunate we need to survive somehow some way don't let time pass you by fight . . .

Above all thinks human needs to love for the subjects that you are going to study in school and make a profession from it freedom of choosing what you like the most and that is going to create your talent why we call it talent because we thought about that subject the most since our childhood and in order to improve our nation and makes it more productive we have to avoid Sexism today in each country who is prospers they never think of a person who is a women or a men it is based on their qualifications on that field of work who qualifies the most will get the job sorry to break the news to you women were more productive than men as statics shown.

Afghanistan should not discharge itself yes we do have enemies don't let it interrupt you from moving forward go with the punches you may get knock down but the only way you lose to stay down get up again take some more punches if it comes death don't ever wary about that I know death scientifically when we die and the soul comes out of our body it's like there is two walls and a roof in side of that room is space and energy that is our soul when those two walls collapse is our body and when we die it's like a telephone line; it has been disconnected temporally what we get a mile. From that point on is space and energy a million miles away from that is again Space and energy. Therefore we never die and the body is like cloths you wear and you change and put on a new form of cloths.

Aging I might be wrong nobody came back from death to tell us what happens when we die that was my Research from scientific point of view may be I went head of myself I might be wrong if I am I apologize. As in our religion Islam god has promised to our prophet Mohammed (peace up on him) that each Muslim will get to go to heaven or paradise that's why this is in our holly book Koran. (Nobody is god but god and Mohammed is his messenger)

In Afghanistan income policy is very important today the government 90% of the time influences the wages prices and profits ranging from milled to direct control the economist who had been using wages and prices has to be carefully in touch with the labor wages because labor economists has to approve the wages and Prices if they do not feel like it does cover dividends means the part of money made by that business which is divided by people who won the share in the business and profits on that note inflation Presets and inflation means the price rising than most of economists will expect and it advocates the wages and advocates means the person who approves send supports an idea in business and price control for everyday life in our country.

Afghanistan has to find a solution to solve the economy issue of her otherwise until when we ask the world for help we need to stand on our own two feet somehow that should be our number one priority of our government we have no choice but to that we cannot be a burden in the globe forever we must shake things up once for all.

To think of security of people and get the fear out of people minds so they can freely function like any other free countries we must collect and canfestecate all of the weapons from people starting from Kabul and all of provinces of Afghanistan we need to have special platoons to do the job to search each individual and each house Collect all the weapons from them if they are hidden in their walls or yards of their houses there is a Special metal detector here in America called (KELLYCO) metal detector and there is hundreds of other kinds of metal detectors I just named one of them should be send to Afghanistan and be used for this very important issue that our nation is suffering from and NATO forces for that matter as well; a country would be dysfunction living in fear every moment when they will be attract or shot at that needs to be taking care of as soon as possible.

Everywhere in the world security of its people is there number one priority; life is too short to live in fear. Confederate as a verb to form an alliance that acts more as a coalition of interests than as a single Sovereignty federate means to form a union to act as one group not as a single unity. Sovereignty a confederation in which each participation power holds onto its sovereignty is weaker than a federation of the political ties that bind the most tightly binding words are union and united then comes federation followed by the loose confederation the association of independent Afghanistan.

There is always conflict of interest the dilemma of a person serves two masters as phrase conflict of interest is relative newcomer to the world; it is as ancient as public servants with private incomes secret holdings or conveniently opinion about the suggestion that an army officer be permitted to maintain with a corporation in which his conflict between the interests of our country and the interests of the corporation and the interests of the army officer as an officer and of the Corporation are more than Likely to arise the justice official qua-toed section the criminal's code and a Statute forbidding government employees from accepting salary from outside sources from government work adding both are intended to prevent conflict between self-interest and the interests of Government the phrase has been added to chapters in the history of our country.

As in this moment that I am writing this book I heard on television that a yang girl at age of fourteen has been shot by Taliban because in that yang age she is an activist and she loves to continue her education in Pakistan by name of Molalla she is fighting for her life in the hospital as we speak I don't know what to make of this as everyone knows Pakistan army doesn't want to stop Taliban; there government wants use them for lots of purposes as I mentioned above they like to keep them for their rainy day.

You get abused; you get frightened you get to adjust yourself with society it seems like outside worlds job is to hart, you judge you and hart you some more the only think are keeping us alive is hope. What kind of feeling is that we are getting fooled by; maybe it's a feeling keeping us going somehow the nature of the beast is there that will never go away doesn't matter how much we try.

A writer writes based on his or her emotions to be intellectual of course the kind of intelligence education and information the writer has to express him or herself if the subject is educational like writing a medical book that is based on the medical books and what he or she have been studying in Medical school but when a writer is writing based on emotions that means that person never found out what kind of talent he or she has in other words never found them self's has a feeling likes to express it based on the pains they have been trough there life's what has been bothering them growing up some of them become a drama writer for movies or wants' to save some one yang and don't want that yang Ester to go through pain and suffering in way the writer wants to save them somehow may be not physically but emotionally and that can be help full for the other people what they are going through so life becomes easy for others.

Every one today is praying for Molalla as she was being transferred by the army helicopter to the hospital and they are not sure if she can survive this heroic head injury as she was unconscionce her beautiful face was shown I saw a light that was angels comforting her that was not an ordinary moment when you have deep senses in some strange way in an extra ordinary moment you can see trough that light or angels you might think I am out of my mind; no you have to pay a deep attention as she was being comforted by a higher power.

Strange patient's god has if I were him on that first moment earth and sky would have been demolished strange patients god has when I see one hand and incent gets hurt and other is the cause of the pain and suffering strange patents god has.

We were talking about future and civilization of our beloved country when we are day dreaming or thinking about something positive to happen to our neighborhoods we have to put it in action because action equals results without action years and years can go by the thoughts are there but there is nothing thoughts it will would be the same situation as we are now.

In nature even a tree by itself take action it grows rapidly as tall as it gets gives us fruit that tree by nature feels responsible and trying to do good for humanity and we are Human the most intelligent being in the surface of the earth what is our responsibility noting but to do good for our own humanity and our own country nobody thinks the same and nobody looks the same even twins has differences and nobody's finger prints are the same in the world that's why each one of us has a different value a different talent that nobody ells has and that uniqueness is cussing the improvement of a nation the parents looks at their chilled what kind of talent he or she has what they like to do the most and they will try their best to provide and to make it possible for them to reach their goal as well as department of education all the way the president of country feels responsible for them.

The theory I am going to talk about is how much our god is involved in in our progress of daily lives everything had to be calculated that means physics intelligence and generally science is involved and that connects our religion and science as they step by step walk with each other in the park.

Most of Scientist of our time asked questions based on mathematics and they found out that religion and since becomes one at the end a theory from the great contest Newton as he says during the first half of the eighteenth century the most important and characteristic interactions between religions and natural Philosophy; occurred in connection with his natural theology several features of which are important to recognize to set the stage for the religious impact of post Newtonian developments in Physics first Newtonian natural theology emphasized the need for some kind of active non material agent either god or something added by god to matter to account for gravitational attraction. To account for gravitational attraction either emphasis continued to support the matter spirit dualism that had emerged as central to Cartesian and corpuscular Philosophy during the seventeenth century the former had special appeal for those who south to find scientific support for beliefs in a god who remained continually active with the natural universe.

Second Isaac Newton insisted that the massively improbable structure of the solar system supported the argument that it had to be the product of a designer god rather than of mere chance. Finally Newtonian natural theology acknowledged indeed it insisted upon the need for gods in frequent but unquestionably miraculous interventions it seemed clear from calculations based on Newton principals that instabilities in the solar system would have caused it to collapse within the duration of beginning in the middle decades of the eighteenth century continuing developments in classical physics undermined the Newtonian position and substantially modified the way in which science and religion were understood to be connected.

As thought makes thinks explanatory as the apple dropped from the tree and Newton was sitting under that tree by thinking deeply he explains the theory of gravity and he makes his research on it made it possible to handstand the power of gravity, and the notion of it again everything comes from write thinking thoughts plus action equals results today time is money in the western world every one moves and moves fast to catch a train or a bus or runs to reach their destination not to just make a living but to reach their dreams or in other words to put things in perspective the way they see it fit and there Government wants to see a shiny temple on the hill regards to their country that's every ones hope and dream as you are driving at two o'clock in the morning you sees lights and police vehicles you are thinking to yourself wow that might be a road block and you are scarred they might test you if you fit to drive you come close and you see they are working on a bridge they have changed the five lane to one lane and they direct you to stay on that one lane as you see there are almost seventy people with shiny uniforms working on that bridge all night and that seventy construction workers are replaced with a new crew and a new energy at eight o'clock in the morning you are thinking to yourself how if that a city never sleeps for improvement would happens to Afghanistan someday somehow god willing.

Every wearer you go you do see conflicts as I grow up here and I have a son from an American Lady who just turned thirteen Sebastian his Mather named him; his Mather has blue eyes and light hair. But Sebastian one 100 present looks like me his mom is a bit joule's about that, but she is the best mother ever and you still feel strange somehow I am a color blind person to me every one is the same but under Neat you feel the hostility from even your own siblings I think this will never change it will go on forever sometimes you see the most power full person try to hurt the weakest without a reason you wonder why this kind of unlawful motion will go on forever I think.

Dally lama is a spiritual leader from Tibet is a small country near the border of china which went under occupation of china in 1940s and dally lama became a refugee in India he is there until today try's to find a solution for his country and china thinks Tibet is a part of china says the best way of life is to be kids again when you are a kid and play you never pay attention to anything ells regardless you just play and you have a sense of comfort without judging each other you just play . . .

In general humans are created to think and have a vision for their own future for their country and above all vision for love that's how life becomes interesting some of you might say I feel like life is tough Sometimes the doors are closed and we have to struggle specially at this historic time of our country for as if we put our mind traditionally in it there is nothing we cannot achieve by the physics we only will get what we ask for anything at all you ask for it the opportunity will represent itself to you if not today you will get it next week as long as the thoughts are there.

If we want to explain that the best way is the scientific way everything has the motion of relativity or cause and effect therefore whatever you feel like to have it represent it to you the difference now obvious predictions for objects moving at very high speed of light but it make a difference these predictions have been experimentally tested on numerous occasions since the theory's inspection and were confirmed by those experiments the first such whether these events occurred before the other major predictions at Special relativity are contradiction along the motion a rad moving with the respect to an observe will be measured to be Shorter than an individual rod at rest and the eqvulance at mass and energy written as E=mc2 special Relativity predicts a liner velocity addition formula which prevents at more geometrical Newton's.

This is how energy and information works together and we create what we create physically and emotionally to establish a reformation in our country Afghanistan we have to be constantly be vigilant and in thatch with both of our senses in order to improve and build our native country again it doesn't matter how money Administration comes, and goes our corporation is needed it's like a professor teach his class and try his best for his class to make it and graduate, but if the students don't fallow he or she will disappoint every one if we don't create our own law, and order doesn't matter how money countries try to come, and establish law and order for us it will not help anything we are the victim of circumstances as we all know and it keeps on makes us look bad somehow we have to creatively get out of it there is no other choice but.

I will do my best to find a way to send machinery for agriculture any think that could be useful for our Nation in this historic time. Except cash money people will make stories out of it.

Some of the country's when it was established like America; luckily they started with great leaders like George Washington Franklyn john Adams, Abraham Lincoln or a brilliant men like Thomas Jefferson who wrote the declaration of Independence and the constitutions law of United States of America which has been practiced until today as they passed the good life possible for the next generations as they moved on with prosperity and developments for the next generations to come and made it possible for the people now to live a good Life that's how leaders with generosity wisdom mature thinking without being selfish made it possible for the next generation to live in comfort in our afghan culture was the opposite I am saying only our own afghan culture hopefully people from other cultures don't take that personally older People without anything to be hopeful about them only did not do anything, but lived good life's in the moment and yang was ignored while everyone knows that chilled someday will do good if he or she been treated Good that's how life works in pros press countries.

Being causation in anybody's personal life is vital because each individual personal life will have a great deal of connection in the future that country causation about choosing our profit ion which we can find out and make sure what we are good at so we don't have to change a career after years of studying in to some ting different and start all over again causation about who we are going to marry causation In each sector of life in theology there has never been any doubt that god can cause things to happen, but there has been a great deal of controversy about the precise nature of god's causative Activity in Nature.

God is undeniably the first or picture as intermediaries underlying differences of theological opinion is differences in the nature of provide naturalism. Voluntarism theologian who provides everything by secondary causes to say that he cannot is to circumscribe his Intellectualist or necessitation theologians who are absolute concept test about causation are prime site for understanding the relationship of our self's with almighty so we have to make cautiously our decisions about our self's, and the future of our country to make possibility's happen as the days and years goes by, we are Lucky our Afghanistan has more stones than any other when our family where going out of Kabul for a picnic I remember those shiny stones at very yang age I was thinking to myself I found some kind of jewelry they were all kinds of colorful stones. And we really can put those stones to use for building our nation with.

Our country's location is and circumstances makes it difficult I would not say impossible as the population grows dramatically in Pakistan today we have 28 million Pashtuns lives in others side of our border with Pakistan called durian; also we have 14 million afghan Pashtuns that 28 million Pakistani Pashtuns wants to mix them with our own native afghan Pashtuns that makes it almost uncontrollable to manage to know who is who I don't mind if they come and go like for the past one hundred years.

But today our country is injured to the core and its people from al-Qaida groups come inside of Afghanistan in The name of Pashtun and at time of our hid celebration explode themselves killing the people while they put on their new cloths on for hid celebration and they are all gathered for hid prayers as they genuinely praying and their eyes are closed making good wishes and asking god for peace and prosperity of Afghanistan they hear an explosion and they all parish as the rummy says again whatever runs in your veins there I feel it here as you have your dinner with your family on that day so called hid you hear the news and you lose your appetite tears in your eyes and you wish you never been born in that country, and there is nothing you can do about that.

Today there is an awakening political domination in the Middle East while there have not been such thing in the past middle east in general Asia in general is awakened and equips them self's with nuclear science which is scaring the world and each one of this country's has some kind of resentment against any authorities who likes to control them, and being in control in the world which they can shake the world with the devastating way if they use their new clear weapons there the Middle East is in the turmoil as we speak their future without a peace full philosophical way and manageable theory will promote this atrocity's as the days goes by. I Believe personally that Taliban is being fund it and being used in Afghanistan so western world to be weekend in other words Asia is saying we will not be crossed by any of western power again the best place is our poor Afghanistan to be used and we pay for that with the incent lives every moment as It goes by today Asia has there conflicts between themselves as well to look at North Korea.

And South Korea, Japan and china Pakistan and India Iran and Israel and the Arab reigns these conflicts will go on as we know for some time to come until they find some kind of compromization to resolve these Issues this country's that I have mentioned they live a good life they are playing chest with their political views and Afghans is the victim of their political gains it doesn't matter to them afghan Blood is cheap today afghan blood feels no more pride afghan blood is nothing, but for use full evil political purposes.

If that is so, New York is not to for from where I live I will go to talk with Mr. Moon of UN enough is enough if necessary I will change him with the reason with someone who knows what they can do for the present world we have to resolve these issues once for all we Afghans are au stages of these countries they are showing off their genus political thinking while we all die so they get what they want there is no remorse for a chilled that lost six member of his family at age of twelve nobody gives a dome . . . as I am screamingly writing this I will do something about it we cannot tolerate this blood shade any more.

We as an afghans and our children are thinking maybe we don't deserve to live may be this is our destiny to die every day we don't deserve to eat we don't deserve to live like any other kids. While those nations are saying greed is good greed for good life greed for money greed for power greed for better future of their children sky . . . . Is the limit how do you feel as an afghan when you are?

Reading this you're blood boils let's put stop to this, Afghanistan will not be used for any ones wars or so called smart moves let's make them handstand that this land is no body's playground no more; Don't even think you will have any future there at any shape or form stops it.

Fundamentalism was created because of science as the scientists created new technology's they kind of ignored the religion all together somehow fundamentalist are for the most part religious descendant's movements that has always taken science seriously. In the early eighteenth century when older forms of religious authority were beginning to give way their religion to their own readings so scripture and to scientific procedures as new supports for their faith there developed as a result a large evangelical.

Evangelical means scullers perching faith is more important than any other study's at that time investment in natural theology and proofs for god for some time these means seemed to work well in coordination religious beliefs and scientific concerns, but from the mid nineteenth century the settled harmonies of earlier days began to give away increasingly scientists seemed not to care about keeping God in the picture more and more Evangelical and their fundamentalist successors thought that some of those who spoke in the name of science were abusing both science and religion the result has been an often tangled twentieth century history of coalition's confrontation cooperation and combat the particular concerns of fundamentalists. And parallel the concerns of many other religious groups in their places and at other times but in and wherever scientific authority is valued these concerns have had an especially volatile relationship with scientific enterprises this is an old cause for fundamental thinking and fundamentalism for clash of science and religion but what kind of science and technology Afghanistan has that fundamentals can get enough of killing our people we are the poorest of poor we didn't create any new technology so fundamentalism would clash with our since as I see it from here they couldn't divide two way streets in Kabul yet you look at the traffic you think they are lost they cannot find their destination where to go to. Science has went on all the way until present time the scientists now says we believe there is an Higher Power is in control we are scientist because we believing in god there is a higher power in control up There we must get our self's out of treat or fundamentalisms issues as soon as we can, and our seculars Job must be preaching kindness, and kindness only, and condemn any kind of terror in the name of our peaceful l religion that must be going on every day.

Anybody who comes from west to rule the country to me is not fair people should choose their leader from within of Afghanistan. The Afghans in the western world who has western education and expertise if they love their country must help in other ways try to open Afghanistan for imports of goods and new technology from the west to Afghanistan they can go and teach they can work for roads and Instruction of bring about new arcitctutrs from west to rebuilt, specially our medical doctors must make rounds for three months if they cannot live there for good and be replaced with the new group of afghan doctors comes from west we have uncountable medical doctors in state of Virginia where I live here in America to help voluntarily that should go round and round for any other Profit ions they have that's what other country's do here they go and help their nation every year.

This form of thinking and responsibilities must be there number one priority in our every year schedule so we can make a difference in our own nation I felt responsible writing this book I was a teenager when I left Afghanistan that's all I remember fighting after class and getting hurt on daily basis this is my memories from Kabul People who had good memories and great pleasures there how they can live with them self's to just stand by and do nothing we live once, and die anyways why not step forward we are not better than anyone ells why not do something our eye is on presidency or have some kind of political power at this time of injured Afghanistan, what a cheap way of thinking that is.

Most of afghan profisnals men and women around the world they are concerned about their safety this issue of security for the people who wants to help their home land this is the very first think they are presenting during their conversations what would happens are we going to be safe if we go home for help, the government of Afghanistan must promise these people that they will be provided security so people don't question that anymore they must feel safe there and their concentration on their duty is important while they are preforming their duty.

Hate what an ugly word there is nothing we can achieve from a negative view in the air as we are gathered there is an energy there is a positive energy, and there is a negative energy depends how we feel that day we are out we feel good we smile that is contages others automatically feel the same in other word if we give a way positive energy we receive positive feet back from that I am not a smiley person never been, but when I feel better I see people feel easy around me, and I can get my work done.

I understand at this time there is numerous problems Afghanistan has we must make the best out of it. We should feel open as much as Islam our religion allow us to get thinks don, at the time beginning of Islam our religion forced the education up on us more than anything ells, at time Baghdad had the biggest library in the world and the constructions, life style of Muslims were so modern and civilized that the entire world was amazed by it as you all know paper what you are writing on was invented in Baghdad. Form of thinking is very important we have so money people without legs or an arm we never should feel or treat them differently be kind to them and respect them Mary them change the way of thinking dramatically today the best scientist our time Stephon Hawkins who is an English man who has been respected for so money years around the world as much as Albert ancetine is limited to a weal Chair he cannot move he cannot dress himself or even feed himself he cannot talk he talk's trough a computer sound system with an American accent, but he is a genus and every one ells feel small around him.

Pull McCarty of beetles who is a famous musician in the globe, he could have any Women, but he falls in love with the women who lost her entire left leg due to an automobile accident and Maries her, so what I am trying to say is a person should have a character, what is character, character is the qualities that makes a person or completes a person that's what character means.

Anyone could not shave or shower and curse the world without reason to me that is ok, but if you want to play with future of a country, and high jack its religion and have a chilled of thirteen years old to have a racket on his Shoulder while he cannot wipe his own nose properly the flies around his nose are gathered for lunch, and he shoots a building killing people and bringing down that building that is not ok . . . .

The world is moving forward at the speed of light we have to catch up with them the world is trying to drug us to the present time, and we are pulling away because of our naïve prejudices it's time to stop that and fallow the caravan that we must.

To talk about present world security and politics of it internationally, today the world has changed there will not be stability If you think about it by Any Perspective, Pakistan is not remaining stable due to all of the conflict in the region there will be a Change of power with respect to ISI Kashmir and Taliban in other corner you can expect a surprise any day there, as America announced that they will leave Afghanistan by 2014 to me is not even imaginable there is so money tribes and war lords are looking forward to that day, America leaving that Region that will be a global Issue and political suside, due to harvesting drugs by war lords, the history basically Repeat it Self again and again that would be out of question US, leaving that region to me is, may be politically we could say Shift of words and some policy, but basically we have to think of the future and what would be the outcome of it.

In order to be a country in that region to be proud of, it might seems difficult at this present time, but if we respect each sector of our land, and above all help the present government to achieve their goals with grace of god we can make it with the respect to mandate on us from our government with invitation of all young educated afghan man and women from whatever they are to pitch in and help with their afghan dignity that they have, most of them has I handstand holding a master's degrees and PHDs we can have a prospers nation I promise you.

How that is going to work out as we are experinasing fatigue from all years of war, and distraction it's like someone is hospitalized you force him to work as a construction worker we need a break we need help if America leaves, and with absence of an effective, and stable government in Kabul, the country would be dominated by rival warlords, and both India, and Pakistan would more assertively and openly compete for influence in Afghanistan with other neighbors also probably involved. As the result, the possibility of at least an indirect war between India, and Pakistan would increase.

Other neighbors will try to exploit Pakistan, and India rivalry in seeking in advantage for itself. Today the world is more defensive and the reason for that is to have an political stability and above all economy stability now days you see how all of the countries are concentrating on their navy and how much money and force they are putting on their waters you see Russians in the black sea India in Indian Ocean and china navy ships are getting stronger now each one has their forces war plans flying and landing on the their navy ships like the movie top gun and they are all are demanding respect, and full control of their waters with combination of nuclear wepen, and power full army's the world is wakened and they are scared nobody wants be scared on that note they want to scare others first in order to feel better pcyclogicaly, there is no love and peace left anymore brothers on a duel with each other it's matter of pride and survival like the old west movies it's called live and lit die, what would be the outcome of that, I believe as a result you will create more and more depressed and an easy society's and each individual must stay on drugs in order to put a day behind, people loves and trust their dogs for Better than each other what's happening to humanity nobody has a bit of mercy on each other when you die they don't say any more he has passed on peace up on his or her soul, they say he is expired like milk in a refrigerator, we are not lucky our parents had it for better life than we do, I call it times of misery that's all. There were times you would create a poem when you were sad and lonely, because you had a bit of Tears left and could express you're self you're motions and feeling, somehow you are so cooled inside, that you can't or read or Liston to a song with poem that you like in it any more as our great composer of our nation fazel hammed, NAYNWAZ while as he losing his close friend the phenomenon musician of our country hammed zhair, simultaneously as he pulls up his salt and paper hair with his deep strong voice with a sad tone sings!

Why my tears in my eyes are circling

    Ho my bloody heart I am asking you, where are those drops

As he was holding the highest degree in political science, a diplomat, and a royal he vanishes from the face of earth without a trace.

Tragedy's goes on, educators of today are predicting Asia and south Asia as they are awakened politically as they are growing economically and as diversity we have they will experience a war between themselves like Europe during early 19th century something god for bed, ignite in Asia like Europe as it happened in world war one, and followed by world war two, therefore I am saying love and cooperation with each other is needed nobody likes us to grow, and be somebody we better watch out otherwise it will be devastating for Middle East, and Asia in general I think diversity is good noting is wrong with that we will learn more from each other we have to take advantage of it in positive way life that way is not boring you always see something different and take advantage of it that is in general in all Asia I am pointing at, but when it comes to our own beloved Afghanistan, when I hear a Pashtun lady speaks in Dari with a bit of an accent I find that very attractive or voicversaw, when I put more pressure in business language I wish it was Pashtu or Dari in international world, but it is in English to be spoken I don't mean anything by it, but we can be able to communicate fluently, and can deal with outside world to do business with, without side world if we want to get somewhere today an Indian yang man or women anywhere are welcomed for employment because the outside world knows their company can do business with them, it doesn't mean that Indian yang person lost his heritage or dignity they go with their accent and customs and make money for their country and establish more possibility for their nation from outside world.

My fellow Afghans pride and prejudice bring us nothing, but to be left Unknown. In the Business world today economy is ruling the worlds and economy only we need to keep up we are not as rich as you aware of, we need to engage our self's in the future with international economy, economic Philosophy we have no choice, but today the internet is being controlled by cyber space in California, and each moment Wall Street in New York every moment the question is how high and low is the stocks and as price of oil, and gold varies the all attention is on economy wye US wants leave on 2012 Because there is an economist and advisors are saying by that date if we go on with same kind of spending we will face an inflation what inflation means you produce less and spend more it is all about finance each solder cost high volume of money as they fight in Afghanistan there will be less army so US can manage the deficit what we afghans are looking for is a comfortable life and that needs financial aids to people in all sectors the time that we can manage to that sari shazada is our stock market looking at them counting the money on the streets while they are setting down, we need economists to have a Serious conversation with them, and change it and change it once for all, fifty years counting money on the floor of that place is enough we need to get a grip on our economy the very first think they need to build stock market, building and latest technology equipment's, in banking finance Industry, Theory and tactics and information credit card projects, a full development of finance in our each Province.

Economy this subject is so important for our nation Afghanistan that is like an air to Breath it's not like old times anymore finance rules and we Afghans must manage to learn the principle of it, and how to grasp it so we able to manage our first problem which has been dominated our nation for so long once for all.

First of all we need to know what we produce how we produce it, and for whom we produce that product, in economy of today as the business tycoon of US Donald trump says when you think you think any ways think big, we must think big when it comes to business and finance in business and economy what we face is numbers and a chart the producing to spending it must circle around itself over and over, economy of any nation never developed itself over night it develops gradually I don't know history of our Poor Afghanistan shows when we get our self's together a little each 60 years some neighbor or Super Power comes and disrupts, and burns Afghanistan to the ground and leaves and that bothers me any ways I must go on with economy at this stage that we are at we must start what causes poverty that can be luck of opportunity it can be luck of job training programs, discrimination on afghan women, and people on drug dependency, now I think this is the basic causes of poverty most of all security and explosions of terror on daily basis, the government role for stabilization of economy is to control the up and downs of business cycles, and increasing, and decreasing the gross of domestic products may be this is out of place here I have read on a some newspaper that the hospitals in western countries can use the drugs afghan Government is burning, and these hospitals wants use those drugs and turn it to medications like Murfree n's and so on and they want to buy them, I don't know if there are any facts in to it or not any ways economy in general is like networking each financial sector has a connection to another they must pass and trade in order to keep on the economy, economy is like a beating heart it must keep on Pumping and being active otherwise you need a surgery I am writing about a subject I don't know anything about, especially when you hear all tragic news about maskers of children here in Connecticut and in Jalalabad I wish I was shot dead instead of them why god is allowing this to take place It hurts me to my core you forget about everything, and your mind goes to a delusion that you can't think Straight and wise may be it is my illness desperation I don't have dry eyes any more tears are Ruling Down out of control you despise life all together, the golden down and beauty of it disrupts itself by the a Storm you see the flashes of the storm it follows with loud lighting as you are scared you see those big trees are falling by that lighting, and loud noise you hear those children we are the golden down we give you the key don't forget me, and you say to yourself my flaming heart and pain of it is forever, floods of my tears are forever ho my moon and stars I love you forever, your eyes are stars in your love, I am hope Less you're the singing birds of garden, and you own it I love you forever,

Life must go on . . .

We were talking about economy, the very basic of economy if we must take a sharp look we will see these sectors to have and follow that will be purpose, creativity, morality, achievement, respect of others, confidence, friendship, family, intimacy, property, health, employment, social stability, water, breathing, food, Sleep shelter -actualization self-esteem, love and belonging, safety physiological the physical infarstusturs of Afghans must follow natural resources including the technology machines and other products that compromise the economy.

But there are other types of capital which are equally essential for meeting the needs recognized when exchanged for real goods and services.

And other plans are essential for meeting the needs, productivity of Afghanistan economy out native plants and animal's geology nutrient, and water flows energy and Natural proses that nature provides, social organizations informal networking market relationships, and most of all trust and constructively enable people to live, and work together in general in capital assets are required to secure economic progress and high quality of life.

Each these capitals are vital and complementary to others. Soil seeds a farmer skills and knowledge social system, such as markets and money that all fits together in the economy to grow food and put it on the a plat, my heandrstanding of my people even when we have the money we don't use it in a productive way, this book is about modernization of Afghanistan we need to develop better taste in clothing furniture choosing of colors for our buildings, and structures of it above all things a respectable social life when a man talks to a girl she should respond in a good manner, and viceversaw we need to develop a trust between each other not to humiliate one and other, we become an adult we expect our parents to choose a love life as well, we need to have command in our own life and for our future so how and what kind of family I am going to have in very logical modernized fashion.

Before we approach in to sector of economy we need to develop, and manage these principles otherwise it doesn't matter how much money we have in our bank accounts it will not be helpful, and we have the money in our pockets, but walking around confused without a goal how to use that money for good productive purpose money is a piece of paper, and has no value we need to distinguish our values first, but the basic and approach towards finance we need to cover the very basic what our needs are it follows.

What a country fundamental human needs are, subsistence physical and mental health food shelter work cloths rest work living environment social setting.

Participation Receptiveness dedication sense of humor responsibilities duties works rights cooperate dissent express opinion association's party's musqs'ks in our neighborhood's affection, respect sense of humor generosity friendship family relationships with nature share take care of, express emotions privacy intimate spaces of togherness.

Understanding, critical capacity curiosity intuition literature teacher's policies educational analyze study mediate investigate schools families universities communities leisure, imagination tranquility spontaneity games parties peace of mind day dream remember relax have fun landscapes intimate spaces places to be alone.

Creation, imagination boldness inventiveness curiosity abilities skills work techniques invent build design work compose interpret sacs for expression workshops audiences.

Identity, sense of belonging self-stem consistency language religions work customs values norms get to know oneself grow commit oneself places one belongs to everyday settings. Freedom, autonomy passion Self-esteem open mindedness equal rights dissent chooses run risks develop awareness anywhere.

This book is for awakening and for modernizing of my nation we must belong to the world we cannot work alone we must become a citizen of the world they learn from us we learn from them in afghan restaurant when an American teats our food like palue or anything ells they ask for their recipes of that dish so the afghan rugs are made by hand it is out of imagination of a westerner so they learn from us they want to know how, so civilization is about people not just technologies, industries, and places. Great resets also involve major population shifts especially in the clustering of what we now refer to as talent our human capital these are times when talent flows out of some places an into others in the case of the first reset this included everyone from farmers looking for better work to inventors migrating farmers and looking for better work to inventors and entrepreneurs seeking new places to launch their enterprises these talent resets thus shift the balance of power among cities and regions as well as among nations locations rise or fall based in their ability to attract retain and productively use talent of all sorts form brilliant innovators to skilled labors.

While reset pushes some regions to the for others decline growing regions grab hold of new technology, and attract new talent, but as these leading regions grow and evolve some eventually fall and committed to old behaviors, and social systems old technologies and even more important out mode, and hard to change institutions organizations, and business practices they are either too slow or literally unable to change this is what set mined growth in manly of the early manufacturing cities in our time technology and new economics systems so often arise in locations that were previously less prominent. In this way economics resets provide the jolt that hastens these geographic shifts above all trust your, self and trust the unknown.

The hardest think is to change that create anxiety's change for the better being afraid of success and attention like your studying, and taking a test and waiting for results waiting for better score like I remember on third or forth grade as chilled at the end of year we were waiting for results so we pass third or fourth grad as I was waiting patiently as the teacher was interring in the class room, and passing the results she was keep calling other class mates name as they passed successfully not mine as I was waiting for twenty minutes with fear and anxiety finally she would have called my name sultan masoud Mash root . . . that was some kind of anxiety I was experiencing as funny it sounds on that day, any ways fluctuations for better, and worse we have to experience, that is how we grow and get better we need to be hopeful keep on trying until the day we die there is no other choice but.

Always positive thinking creates better wellbeing and economy, westerners always try to exchange positive results from a negative thinking negative motion stops economy, and anything creative for example when you are in negative thoughts you are angry you get in the room and try to turn on the lights because of negative motion you have in you the lamp burns out and you have to change the light bulb so as well you Start your car with negative motion the engine won't start because the negative energy and Motion is in the air and even an mechanical machine will feel it that's how positive thinking create and Make possible good energy and creativity for better life as well more possibilities and wealth and good ness, mathematical thinking is important not only for creativity of anything not just for build buildings and Bridges is vital for creating and possibilities, otherwise something is missing we don't know What, but something is missing and it doesn't look good, and you wonder why as the motion and energy decreases and increases like animals in sea we have to go with flow otherwise we face a dead lock, and we can't move forward as they say attract like attract you are attracted to a girl and motion flashes a million miles away in matter of minutes and feel it in you she likes you back that is cosmos as it flashes in speed of sound and god is in between that's how we feel alive and hopeful it makes life interesting and a predictable in this is another way I am describing possibilities for creative thinking as America landed on the moon in 1963 very basic few things was involved creative thinking positive thinking Mathematics and motion that made it possible to land on the moon for the first time the same thing for creating better economy we have to follow that motions as our president karzi traveling around the world he is trying to establish the base the base is have enough wealth in Afghanistan banks in order to establish possibilities for afghan people to reach the employment to have a stable health centers as well as army and so forth for one person to do that kind of work, and we watch and judge that is a crime we need to know our responsibilities as an afghan citizen when we see a small tree that is not stable or about to fall we need to do something about it so that three should grow as it should be, and that tree doesn't have to be in our own yard to fix it, it can be a small tree outside while you went out for a walk or exercise if we don't manage our self the world is laughing at us and they make remarks that you don't want to hear it, we must establish a good economy it doesn't matter how we need to make it possible for our children for our self and the future of Afghanistan if we don't know how we must read about it learn it from others that we must to lay the plans and determine the strategy for the winning of a lasting peace and the establishment of Afghanistan higher than ever before known we cannot be content no matter how high that general standard of living may be if some fraction of our people whether it is one third or one fifth or one tenth is ill fed ill clothes ill-housed and insecure. Afghans must begin to grow and develop strength under the protection of certain inalienable political rights among them we must expand our industrial economy, and come to a realization to fact that true individual freedom cannot exist without economic security and independence people who are angry and out of job are the stuff of which the stuff of dictatorships are made.

Adequate food and clothing and recreation large and small trade in atmosphere of freedom from unfair competitions and domination by monopolies at home and abroad the write of every family for a decent home to live in and the opportunity to achieve and enjoy good health protection and not have economic fears of old times, and establish a good education environments and work force contributing the programs that make for a more capable labor force an provide greater opportunities and security for ordinary workers to earn success in various and giving that worker to learn and grow and let them to express their artistic creativity's that will be an investment for us, and good low cost child care as well as give the mothers to contribute to the world of work outside home.

Today the world is in other stage it is for richer and resourceful than ever before by stroking a key you can get any info that you desire and at the same time we are facing paradox, paradox means a statement which seems to be impossible these success as humans reached today endangering the humanity there is nearly 7 billion people in the world who all need resources the land temperatures are keep on rising flood seacoasts spread tropical diseases agriculture, system already occupies 24 percent of the earth land area global fresh water shortages are rapidly escalating, the world oil production is decreasing, more than twenty countries are now deforested, hurricanes are larger and more frequent and harmful industrial chemicals are found in every human beings body, world food prices are rising while one billion people remain malnourished, yes ladies and gentleman we are not living in a stable world any more we need to watch out for the future of Afghanistan each sector of our nation must be nourished, and make it possible to last longer for the next generations to come, each country the very first thing they demand is there own benefits that's how it should be why nobody paid much attention to Afghanistan a decade ago because there were not much fear of terror on that scale, this is a chance for us to survive as they say use it or lose it, lets embrace it lets protected let's take that land to the next level and have afghan children to reach all fundamental needs for ever, don't ever be afraid of Taliban again after 2014 if they come for occupation again there is Indian Ocean the worlds Navy fighter gets are parked there they will bomb the heck out of them that much I know. Let's move on with better economy most of the time economist has strategies they sell their companies while have Strong values they get a grip to get stronger market at the expense of failing competitors including acquiring them cheaply and they sell the parts of their business that are least strategic long term, and use the proceeds to acquire assets market share, and companies in the areas best positioned for long term trends during the downturn mostly.

The business sectors for better economy start with innovation, innovation means the development of something new from *1%* they make it influential they step to 10% in early majority jump on 50% to late majority of 99% this is the principle of most fundamental forecasting tools for developments of products markets, and innovation and the trend of following appears to occur in financial markets as different levels of participants from sophisticated traders to institutional managers to everyday investors, and they move progressively to bull market that means they raise their prices so basically that's how they begging to start a company and make profits, we need to realize that a business will be conducted in three stages your company your customers and your competitors we need to know what is your company going to do, what products or services will it provide how big or small would it be retail or wholesale where will it be located how can you best position yourself.

Who will your customers be will you be selling to other businesses or to individuals are your customers how big is the market what your potential customers needs are why they buy it from you what do they want would they pay for it what do they read and watch the, more you crystallize your thinking the more Specific you are about who you are trying to reach and the more you know about that market the greater chance that you will be able to find and entice them to patronize your business, patronize means as act towards better who will be your competitors what are they doing right and wrong, what are their strengths and Weaknesses how can you capitalize on their weaknesses why would their customers leave, and come to you can you undersell them do you want to, the reason I am writing more about establishing a business to grow the economy I believe that is now number one problem in Afghanistan our country when economy gets better people is a bit comfortable other things will fall in place naturally.

Starting a business from scratch is a daunting task. You must do everything right, from picking the right business, to giving it the right name, to finding the right location and lease, to getting a business license and in assurance and that is just for starters. It is no wonder that many budding business owners optimistic to buy an existing business.

Buying someone else's business has several advantages. Firth you will not be starting from scratch the business already exists. Second you will not have to create goodwill a favorable reputation in the community that important aspect as already been handled by the current owner. Third it is quicker everything should already be in place to hit the ground running. But the main benefit of buying an existing business is that it reduces your risk. A wise man once said that an entrepreneur is a person who is willing to take a risk with money to make money to make money. As I mentioned there is no guarantee that you will make money to make money. A buy sinless risk, a calculated business risk, but notice that I said a calculated business risk. Remember great entrepreneurs are not gamblers rather they seek to reduce risk as much as possible. Another way to do that is to buy an established business such businesses have a rack record, you look at the books see how much money it made during the past few years, and have pretty good idea of how much it will make next year. You simply do not have that sort of information or comfort when you create a business from scratch.

The other option is get in to incubators, incubators means low cost option to start your business in a business incubator business incubators are partnerships among public private, and nonprofit organizations that work to promote entrepreneurship, and small business growth. They do this by providing inexpensive sake from which new businesses can be launched. Incubators usually offer free or very inexpensive administrate service assistance, legal help business planning financial advice and so forth, as the name indicates they are places that nurture or incubate a business while it learns to spread its wing's and flies.

Most of the time a business must create cash flow; cash is like oxygen for the business without it will Suffocate and die.

One more reason to create a budget then is to ensure that you will have adequate cash flow, I can't say this anymore plainly without consistent, sufficient money to buy inventory, pay bills, handle fending your cash flow, and so forth.

You have compute or calculate your profitability the concept that profit is easy to understand, it is the difference between what it costs you to make or buy your product, and what you earn from selling it, it is when you break down this seemingly simple concept that things get a little complicated? When comes to profit there are four components to understand gross profit, net profit, margin, and markup, markup means by amount of product which the price has raised up at this point we must think of gross profit and net profit the gross profit on a product like kharbooza sold or service rendered is computed by taking the money you brought in from the sale, and subtracting the cost of goods sold net profit is your gross profit, less taxes and interest.

If you a have company and you hire more than 200 employees, you need to know people work for money Reasons and compensations is just one of those reasons, compensations means to give back like a reward or to have insurance in case of an accident and so forth. To create and sustain a successful small business, you need to take into account the money benefits that people derive from work; they desire to make a difference by giving you good services, what you need to provide for them is to create a condition to foster happy productive work place. For our nation at the stage that we are at after all wars and so forth, we need to develop really smart training techniques people needs it if you properly train this new generation to be successful in business we just cannot go by lectures alone, we need to shadow sending people to action with already trained employees are fast way to get the Afghans get in to speed.

Videos, People recall what they see videotapes can be a very effective training method for employees as well as managers video training can teach people how to sell how to open the business, and how to close the bissness the internet on line if the need to know can be very helpful for booming the businesses if they want to know how or have staff members contribute sells calls and success stories to the class to use as Examples. I am putting values and time for economy learned from the classes I took, because I think number one problem is our low economy when you cannot afford to pay for your needs that causes anger, and so money other atrocities as diverse afghan nation are low economy cusses us to be divided not united. Another way of making money is to work at home you can make a contract with company, and do their work at home, but needs requirements you need to have space at home to create a private office, and be self-disciplined enough to work when your family is around, you need technology requirements to run a modern home based business, a separate phone line, computers, high speed internet, cell phone and fax machine you need to cut off from colleagues darning work time stay away from loud noises babies, and Family needs to respect that leave you alone during your work time. Another form of making profit is to barter, barter means to exchange good for goods there are two forms of barter using the traditional method you and another vendor agree to trade goods or services. More often these days barter is done through barter exchange issues barter bucks to you when you do something for someone else in the country. You can then use those bucks to purchase goods or services from anyone else in the company in need, Barter exchanges have cropped up around the world, and they are great places of small businesses to exchange goods, and do business with.

Big businesses for better developments, and continues good income and economy for our nation Afghanistan is to know the successes factors, and they are management with unusual vision, and commitment to meritocracy, meritocracy means a social system which gives the highest positions to people with most ability, hiring and nurturing the best, and the brightest for a world class work force, and corporate culture stressing integrity, imagination, and speedy adaption as well as an uncompromising focus on process discipline, and solid diversified client relationships with high retention or facts in mind to promote Afghanistan's needs for better economy, unusually well corporate governance, and Transparency or clear vision.

Today in US most of our Afghans are working in financial sectors like banks insurance companies world bank all the way to it's management when I was working in hotel management my bosses was telling me that our meddle eastern employees are very good with money; I believe afghans are having a special talent when it comes to finance. If they can manage it here they can manage it in our own nation Afghanistan as well.

We need to network, networking means a large system of wires lines tubes crosses, and meet one another I believe this is the best way of promote our economy the purpose of networking is to team up with other business they are all the same customers who you have some synergy, with write strategic partner, you can combine, and leverage for little extra money your respective distribution networks infrastructure and knowledge for greater success the team work works for example from Kabul entitle cross promoting to Herraat at first you see if the other business congruent with yours, do you have the same goals yon need to discuss, and agree on the purpose of the partnership, and what each side expects, what are the downsides to deal brainstorm both the positive and negative, is the deal a win win negotiate viable commitments that both sides what is the exit strategy having a set of definable objectives allows you to know when the partnership is, and not working what will trigger, and end to the deal there on other side. Now there is golden chance for us to dig out our oil Gus and most of our natural resources, since the world attention are on us now possibly we can built facility's for production of our natural resources like Oil Gus coal valuable stones, and so forth like other countries in our reign, so we can establish the economy from the Ground up, and survive, when western country's help us develop these productions they actually help them self's in a long run.

May be if we fallow this path when we get there
                    It would be a time to sing the poem of happiness

On that note I am closing this book, this book that I have been rten is a gift for my nation, I don't get a dime from it, as child as you run home cause its getting dark, you see a massive magnificent gold painting like on dark blue sky, and you ear a magical voice from the mask . . .

Nobody is god, but god, and Mohammad is his messenger . . .

Mohammed Naim Nawabi
famous football player during 1950's

www.ingramcontent.com/pod-product-compliance
Lightning Source LLC
Chambersburg PA
CBHW050420290526
45786CB00003B/1345